If I'm
in charge
here
why is
everybody
laughing?

If I'm in charge here why is everybody laughing?

by David Campbell, Ph.D.

CENTER FOR CREATIVE LEADERSHIP
P.O. Box 26300
Greensboro, North Carolina 27438-6300 U.S.A.

Acknowledgements

Excerpts from the following sources appear in this volume:

Doris Kearns, *Lyndon Johnson and the American Dream,* Copyright ©1976. Reprinted by permission of Harper & Row Publishers.

Freeman Dyson, "Disturbing the Universe: Part II" in *The New Yorker* August 13, 1979. Reprinted by permission.

Winston Churchill, *The Gathering Storm.* Copyright © 1948 by Houghton Mifflin Company and renewed 1976. Reprinted by permission of Houghton Mifflin Company.

Golda Meir, *My Life.* Reprinted by permission of G. P. Putnam's Sons. Copyright © 1976.

Two quotes from *Conversations with Kennedy* by Benjamin C. Bradlee. Copyright © 1975 by Benjamin C. Bradlee. Used by permission of W. W. Norton & Company, Inc.

Mutual Accommodation: Ethnic Conflict and Cooperation by Robin M. Williams, Jr. Copyright © 1977 by the University of Minnesota. Reprinted by permission of the University of Minnesota Press, Minneapolis.

The Doctors Mayo by Helen Clapesattle. Copyright © 1941 by the University of Minnesota. Used by permission of the University of Minnesota Press, Minneapolis.

Boss: Richard J. Daley of Chicago by Mike Royko, Copyright © 1971, E. P. Dutton. Reprinted by permission.

Winston Churchill, *Triumph and Tragedy.* Copyright © 1953 by Houghton Mifflin Company. Reprinted by permission of Houghton Mifflin Company.

John Kenneth Galbraith, *Ambassador's Journal.* Copyright © 1969 by John Kenneth Galbraith. Reprinted by permission of Houghton Mifflin Company.

Lady Bird Johnson, *Lady Bird Johnson: A White House Diary,* Copyright © 1970. Reprinted by permission of Holt, Rinehart, & Winston.

American Caesar by William Manchester, Copyright ©1978. Reprinted by permission of Little, Brown and Company.

"Defender of the Dollar." Reprinted by permission from *Time,* The Weekly Newsmagazine; Copyright © 1979 by Time Inc.

The Powers that Be by David Halberstam. Reprinted by permission of Alfred A. Knopf, Inc. Copyright © 1979.

Wind, Sand, and Stars by Antoine de Saint-Exupery, 1967. Reprinted by permission of Harcourt Brace Jovanovich, Inc.

"What's an Entrepreneur?" by Berry Gordy In *The New York Times,* January 14, 1979. Copyright © 1979 by The New York Times Company. Reprinted by permission.

Cover Design by Gene Tarpey
Illustrations by Dusty Rumsey
SECOND EDITION
Copyright © 1980
David P. Campbell

Printed in the United States of America.

Center for Creative Leadership
P.O. Box 26300
Greensboro, NC 27438-6300 U.S A.
International Standard
Book Number: 0-912879-90-4
Library of Congress
Number: 79-57376

0 9 8

Contents

Foreword

The title of this book had a very specific birth:

On my fifth anniversary as Vice President of the Center for Creative Leadership, my subordinates "honored" me with a David Campbell Celebrity Roast. It was a wonderful evening. The cafeteria was set with red-checkered tablecloths and candles, the ambience was mellow, the mood light and laughing. Person after person paraded to the podium to offer sly jibes and friendly teasing. As the spirits flowed, the punch lines flew faster. We have a creative group, and after one particularly devastating series of injokes, with everyone doubled over in laughter at my expense, I looked out over the audience and thought wryly, "If I'm in charge here, why is everybody laughing?" I was working on this book at the time, and I immediately knew that that had to be the title.

This is a good place to publicly thank all of those who have made the last five years of my life such a remarkable experience . . . and, as I say that, why are you smiling?

David Campbell
1980

*Sex is engaging in the first rounds;
what sustains interest in the long run
is power.*

Chiang Ch'ing
Chinese actress and wife
of Mao Tse-Tung
(*Time*, March 21,1977)

I

The Upward Spiral of Leadership

Here are three things you should know about leadership.

It Is Demanding

Leadership is frequently frustrating, chaotic, and unappreciated. Different people pull you in different directions; there is never enough money in your budget; your social life is disrupted; having responsibility for others can keep you awake long into the night; no one else quite understands the stress you are under. Being in charge is a challenging assignment.

It Is Enriching

You can constantly grow through a series of expanding challenges; you can master new skills, study more involved concepts, gather broader experiences, meet a wider circle of friends, and develop bigger plans for the future. At every leadership level, there are personal improvements you can make, and the cumulative result is an enriched life.

It Can Be Exhilarating

To be a successful leader—to walk into turmoil and make something good out of it—is one of life's most satisfying, even exhilarating, activities. Not only are the emotional rewards wonderful, the cash may not be all that bad either.

Antarctic Survival

On October 29, 1915, a group of tattered Antarctic explorers gathered together in a small knot on a frozen ice pack in the Weddell Sea. Their situation was desperate. Nine months earlier, their ship, the Endurance, had been trapped, frozen in, immobilized. Since then, they had drifted helplessly, floating in a huge, clockwise circle. Their only hope lay in the possibility that the ice floe containing their ship would eventually be forced to the edge of the pack and expelled once more into the open sea.

That hope proved futile. Two days earlier, the sea had finally ground the ice into a tight pincer clamp around their ship, crushing its sides and letting the sea pour in. The ship would float for four more weeks, but it was now uninhabitable and slowly sinking.

They were hopelessly marooned. No one knew where they were. They had no radios, snowmobiles, helicopters, nor any other modern equipment. They did have seventy sled dogs, a substantial supply of food, three twenty-two foot lifeboats ... and Sir Ernest Shackleton, the most indomitable polar leader of all time.

Shackleton called the group together on the ice. He told them that their only hope, now that their ship was sinking, was to drag the lifeboats over the almost impassable ice pack to the open sea—some 350 miles—and then to sail them 1000 miles to the nearest civilization through the roughest seas on the globe.

S.S. ENDURANCE

He emphasized that they must travel light. Each man could keep the clothes on his back, two pairs of mittens, six pairs of socks, two pairs of boots, a sleeping bag, a pound of tobacco, and two pounds of personal gear.

In a dramatic end to the briefing, Shackleton reached into his clothes, took out some gold coins, hefted them momentarily, then flung them away into the snow. Finally, he took out his Bible given to him by Queen Alexandria, tore out the Twenty-third Psalm and the flyleaf with her inscription on it, folded them carefully into his pocket, laid the Bible gently in the snow, and walked away.

The next day they started. There would be thirteen months more of danger, starvation, thirst, and freezing hardships before they would be saved, but they would survive because of the powerful leadership of Ernest Shackleton.

Shackleton's life is a wonderful adventure story (he eventually died in the Antarctic), and his career is a clear illustration of one of the most important themes in the lives of most leaders: the upward, ever-expanding spiral that most of them take on the way to their greatest accomplishments.

The Spiral

The leadership spiral can begin early in almost anyone's life. Usually it has three components and happens something like this:

First, you get some experience. You are wandering along through life, doing your job, remaining alert as events flow past you. You learn new skills, make new friends, gain more education, collect experiences. Then one day, without realizing it, you take on some mild new responsibility and a new direction begins to appear, faint at first, so fragile that it may disappear into other interests. Other, new, will-o'-the-wisp directions appear along the way, but sooner or later one sticks and you become involved in something that holds your interest.

You can let this process just happen, bumbling along through it, never thinking about the patterns in it, or you can organize your experiences, take some initiative, and impose your will upon the shape of your life. You can speed up the process of collecting experiences by trying a wider range of activities, by learning a wider range of skills, by meeting more and different types of people, by taking some risks, by learning that a few failures are not catastrophic and that even they give you more experience. As a sportswriter once said, "A few early failures in life take the pressure off of trying to maintain an undefeated record."

Second, you learn to be creative, to do things slightly differently from the people around you. You see where improvements can be made, where changes can be useful. Perhaps you find a better way to organize a collection you have started, or a more interesting way to lay

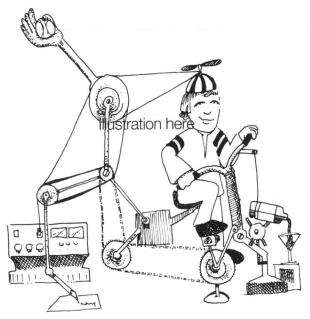

out the set in a one-act play you're in, or a more efficient system of organizing your group's accounting methods. You put some energy, however modest, into changing something, based on the experience you have accumulated, and you are—voilà!—**CREATIVE.**

Everyone goes through the first phase, that of gaining experience—that happens to you every morning when you get up to face the world—but not everyone has the advanced ability to see where improvements can be made. Yet it is not difficult. To see where small changes in procedure might help, to imagine minor improvements in the materials you are working with, to try out slight modifications of schedules is not really that hard—but most people don't bother.

Why not?

I don't know.

But I do know that with even a modest amount of training, the kind available in creative problem-solving institutes or innovation training sessions, most people can be helped to expand the way in which they look at the world. Once you have some experience, you should concentrate on doing something different with it; if you do, you will stand out from the pack, ready for the third phase in the upward spiral.

Third, you take charge. After you have collected some experience and can see how to use it creatively, you will probably want an opportunity to be in charge, to make different things happen, to be a leader.

Interestingly, when you go through these three steps in some project:

Experience (accumulating knowledge)
Creativity (changing directions)
Leadership (making it happen)

you will find that you now have more experience, which you can follow with greater creativity, which requires more leadership, all of which lead you into the ever-expanding upward spiral of leadership. Each conquered challenge leads to more experience (plus some necessary self-confidence), grander ideas, and more demanding, rewarding leadership opportunities.

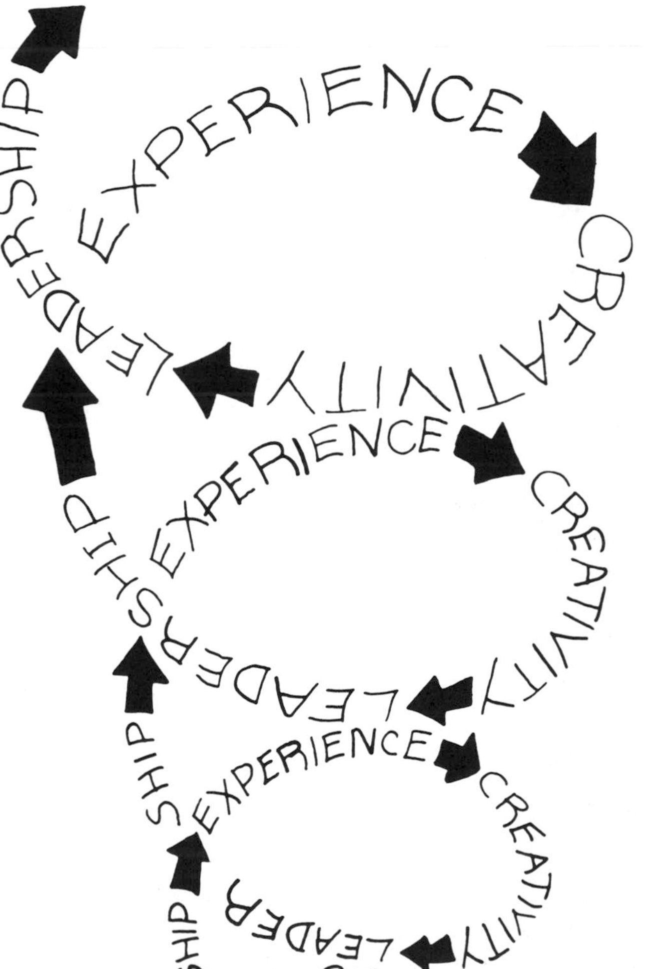
EXPERIENCE
CREATIVITY
LEADERSHIP
EXPERIENCE
CREATIVITY
LEADERSHIP
EXPERIENCE
CREATIVITY
LEADERSHIP
EXPERIENCE
CREATIVITY
LEADERSHIP
EXPERIENCE
CREATIVITY
LEADERSHIP
EXPERIENCE
CREATIVITY
LEADERSHIP

But I am repeating myself, which is exactly the point. Leadership is a repeating cycle, starting small, growing big.

Ernest Shackleton's life was an excellent example of this spiral. He first went to the Antarctic in 1901 as a junior officer under Robert Scott. He returned six years later in charge of his own expedition, attempting unsuccessfully to reach the South Pole. He made it to within ninety-seven miles of the Pole, closer than anyone had ever been, but ran out of supplies and had to return to the coast. The Norwegian explorer Roald Amundsen reached the Pole in December, 1911, before Shackleton could organize another attempt (followed thirty days later by Scott, who was bitterly disappointed not to have been first. The disappointment turned into tragedy; Scott and his crew starved to death on their way back to the base camp.)

As both Amundsen and Scott had reached the Pole, Shackleton wanted to do something more dramatic, so in 1914, he decided to walk across the entire Antarctic continent, roughly 1,000 miles. He failed when his ship was trapped in the ice before he even reached shore, but his resourcefulness in bringing his party safely home after being marooned for twenty months insured his place in history.

The upward spiral of leadership can be seen in the life patterns of leader after leader, people who have dominated their fields in politics, business, the military, even the arts. Here are two

more brief examples to illustrate the point—
one from politics, one from the world of art.

Lyndon B. Johnson:
Our 37th President

On November 22, 1963, Lyndon B. Johnson crowded into a small cabin of the President's plane, Air Force 1, with his staff, his family, reporters, and Mrs. John F. Kennedy, to be sworn in by Judge Sarah Hughes as the 37th President of the United States. He succeeded the late John F. Kennedy, who had just been assassinated.

Johnson returned to Washington and led the U.S. Congress through one of its most active phases in American history; Johnson, at least in his own eyes, gave us "more laws, more houses, more medical services, more loans, and more promises to people than any other President in history." (Doris Kearns, *Lyndon Johnson and the American Dream*, 1976.) While the Vietnam War was to mark an unfortunate and abrupt end to his political career, his impact on this country has been huge and enduring.

His career was tailored to place him at the pinnacles of power. He began learning the political process early as a student at San Marcos College, a teachers college in southwestern Texas.

Doris Kearns, in her excellent biography, describes his start.

"In the first month, he studied the structure of the college. . . . Freshman Johnson wanted to know precisely how things worked, who made them work, what activities to join, what courses to take, which professors to seek out—all with a view to recognition, achievement, and a maximum control over this new environment."

By the time he left San Marcos, he was comfortably in charge as the Student Body President, a major force to be reckoned with on campus.

In his first job his propensity for creating change continued. As an elementary school principal in Cotulla, Texas, he immediately began organizing. He introduced spell-downs, public speaking tournaments, and sporting events, at first working only with the children, then inviting the parents, and finally arranging field days with a wide range of neighboring schools.

From Cotulla he moved on to Washington as a member of a Texas Congressman's staff. Once again, his first activity was learning how the strings of power were intertwined within the organization; as Kearns describes him, "He wanted to take apart the clock of the congressional world in order to discover what made it tick and how each of the many tiny pieces fit together." He learned so well that at age twenty-three he became the youngest Speaker in the history of the Little Congress, a mock Congress composed of congressional staff members.

When President Roosevelt established the National Youth Administration in 1935, Johnson became the youngest State Director in America, and "in six months, eighteen thousand young Texans were at work building parks, constructing buildings, painting murals, planting grass, repairing school buses, sewing clothes, surveying land, and laying bricks" (Kearns).

He was clearly on the upward spiral.

The remainder of Johnson's career followed the same pattern. Each step became a learning plateau for his next level of achievement. At age twenty-nine, he was elected to Congress. In 1943 he bought the Texas radio station which became the basis for his personal fortune. In 1948 he was elected to the U.S. Senate. In 1951 he became party whip. In 1953 he became the Senate Democratic Party Leader, which at the time was minority leader. In 1955 he became Senate Majority Leader, in 1960 Vice President, and in 1963 President, at which time he focused his awesome experience, creativity, and leadership skill into remaking our society. But for the unexpected tragedy of Vietnam, he would probably be remembered as one of our most effective presidents.

Unfortunately, the Vietnam involvement was Johnson's first step into international politics, and he had no time to learn through the spiral. If he had had some earlier experience overseas, he might have recognized earlier what a painful dilemma Vietnam would prove to be for the United States. As it was, his leadership spiral prepared him superbly, but only for domestic politics.

Alexander Calder: Our Most Visible Sculptor

A third example of the leadership spiral appears in the career of the sculptor, Alexander Calder, who introduced us to the world of stabiles and mobiles, these wonderful, light, moving, airy works of art.

Calder, in his later years, produced some of the most visible art in America: a huge mobile in New York City's John F. Kennedy Air Terminal, a bright red, black, and blue one in the dramatic East Building of the National Gallery of Art in Washington, D.C., and—the most mobile piece of art in history—Braniff Airline's 707 jet airplane, painted in contemporary patterns by Calder.

Calder did not start out constructing huge, dramatic sculptures; like leaders in other endeavors, he worked up to it, starting small, constantly experimenting, trying new approaches. He began as a draftsman, took a degree in mechanical engineering, worked as a newspaper artist, and made circus toys before concentrating on metal sculpture. Simply scanning a partial listing of his accomplishments illustrates the expanding nature of his production:

1898—Born in Lawnton, Pennsylvania
1919—Graduated with Mechanical Engineering degree
1919-23—Worked as a draftsman and engineer; traveled
1923—Took first job as an artist—for the National Police Gazette
1925—Received commission to decorate a sports equipment store
1926—Created circus animals in wood and wire
1928—First showing of wire sculpture
1929—Exhibition of wood sculpture
1930—Began experimenting in abstract art
1931—First exhibit of stabiles
1932—First exhibit of mobiles
1939—Won Plexiglas contest
1940—Jewelry exhibit
1946—Paris exhibit of large and small mobiles
1954—Installed mobiles in Beirut and Israel
1955—Installed mobiles in Germany
1958—Installed mobiles in Brussels
1965—"Big Sail" stabile, forty feet high, twenty-five tons, installed at M.I.T.
1967—"Man" stabile, eighty tons, installed in Montreal
1968—"Les Trois Pics" erected in Grenoble, France for the 1968 Winter Olympics
1969—"Gwenfritz" installed at the Smithsonian; "La Grande Vitesse" in Grand Rapids, Michigan; "Moving Cobweb," a huge, walk-through stabile erected in St. Paul de Vence, France
1976—Painted Braniff's Bicentennial plane
1976—Calder's death
1978—His largest mobile, seventy feet long, 900 lbs. of aluminum, hung in the new East Building of the National Gallery of Art

Even with this remarkable record of achievement, Calder was continually striving for improvement. A newspaper reporter covering the unveiling of the Braniff plane in 1976 reputedly saw Calder gazing up at the plane, his newest achievement, muttering wistfully to himself, "I still have so much to learn . . ."

The lives of these three men illustrate the components of the upward spiral—experience, creativity, and leadership. All three men—Shackleton, the polar explorer; Johnson, the politician; Calder, the artist—continually went through the three phases, always moving upwards.

Without these phases, life can be bland, never changing. Everyone accumulates experience; that is no problem. But many people with twenty years of experience simply repeat one year's experience twenty times; they make no forward progress because the second and third steps—creativity and leadership—require more energy. These steps are worth it though, because the dessert course in life comes from thinking up ways to change, improve, and expand that portion of the world you are experienced in, and then making new things happen. The results are pleasant—a sense of growth, greater freedom, a feeling of relevance, a belief that what you do matters—and that is heady wine. Making a living is necessary and often satisfying; eventually, making a difference becomes more important.

But patience, it takes time, as demonstrated in the following passage from Winston Churchill's memoirs.

"Presently a message arrived summoning me to the Palace . . . I was taken immediately to the King . . . He looked at me searchingly and quizzically . . . and said, "I want to ask you to form a Government." I said I would certainly do so.

"Thus, then, on the tenth of May (1940), at the outset of this mighty battle, I acquired the chief power in the State, which henceforth I wielded in ever-growing measure for five years and three months of world war . . . .

"During these last crowded days of the political crisis, my pulse had not quickened at any moment. I took it all as it came. But I cannot conceal . . . that as I went to bed at about 3 a.m., I was conscious of a profound sense of relief. At last I had the authority to give directions over the whole scene. I felt as if I were walking with Destiny, and that all my past life had been but a preparation for this hour and for this trial . . . I thought I knew a good deal about it all, and I was sure I should not fail. Therefore, although impatient for the morning, I slept soundly and had no need for cheering dreams. Facts are better than dreams."

Winston Churchill
The Gathering Storm
Houghton Mifflin Co., 1948

II

What Are Leaders Like?

"He had a talent for self-dramatization, an ability to project to his audience an image larger than life . . . Again and again in the reminiscences of Los Alamos veterans, we read how Oppenheimer communicated to the whole laboratory a personal style that made the enterprise run in harmony, like an orchestra in the hands of a superb conductor."

Freeman Dyson
"Disturbing the Universe: Part II"
The New Yorker
August 13, 1979
Speaking of Robert
Oppenheimer, the physicist
who directed the develop-
ment of the first atomic
bomb.

There have been many psychological studies of people in leadership positions. The results show that, compared with other people, leaders:

- are bright, alert, mentally agile, intelligent
- seek responsibility, enjoy taking charge
- are skillful at whatever they are leading in and, in addition, are administratively and

socially competent
- are energetic, active, durable
- are good communicators; they can speak or write clearly and forcefully

Like all generalizations about human behavior, these are not completely true in all cases. Exceptions can easily be found, especially as the importance of each characteristic varies from situation to situation, yet research and practical experience continue to document their validity.

Leaders Are Bright, Mentally Agile, Alert People

Intelligence is the capacity to handle complex mental tasks, to see relationships between apparently unrelated objects, to see patterns in murky information, to draw accurate conclusions from chaotic data. Leaders are often faced with intricate problems: planning complex schedules, overseeing complicated budgets, or making decisions quickly with only a few data points. A few dumb mistakes are seldom critical, but if you continue to pull bonehead plays day in and day out, you will not stay long in a position of power.

"When you are the Commanding Officer of a large aircraft carrier, sitting in the middle of a brewing storm with the wind picking up and waves running high, and 20 aircraft circling

overhead awaiting instructions as to how to land,
only one thing is important about your decision
. . . it had better be right."
Admiral Noel Gayler
Commanding Officer,
Aircraft Carrier *Ranger*

Can intelligence be taught? Can you make yourself brighter to become a better leader? This is an interesting question, one on which you will find violent disagreement between experienced psychologists who have studied this issue for years. My own analysis is that the general range of our intelligence is fixed by genetic and early childhood factors, but within that range practice, education, and continual training can make a difference.

Probably it is a little like high jumping. If you went out to a track meet this afternoon you would probably do well to jump over a bar as high as your waist—yet the world's record is about two feet over your head. If you went into an intensive training program, you could undoubtedly improve drastically, raising the bar gradually to new heights, but eventually you would find some upper limit above which you could not jump, no matter how long and hard you trained. Then to stay at that upper limit, you would have to stay in shape and continue to practice daily.

Because we are not often faced with the challenge of physically jumping over things, most of us don't train as high jumpers or worry much about improving that skill.

Intelligence is another matter. If you wish to continually advance, to jump hurdles of increasing complexity, to stay mentally alert and agile, then you have to stay in condition by reading, studying, accepting new mental challenges, seeking stimulating education and training courses, testing your current ideas and thinking up new ones. For those in leadership positions, mental stretching should be a way of life.

Leaders Seek Out Responsibility

"Unless a capacity for thinking be accompanied by a capacity for action, a superior mind exists in torture."
Benedetto Croce

The capacity for action shows up in personality traits such as dominance and self-confidence, and in actions such as taking charge and making things happen.

Explaining how leaders take charge is not easy. It probably happens in at least two ways. First, there may be truly dominant people with both the need and necessary skills to be in charge, to take responsibility, and to make things happen. These are the "born leaders."

Second, more commonly, there is the upward spiral quality in the career progressions of most people who hold leadership positions. They begin early in life to migrate into leadership roles: class president, athletic team captain, scout leader. If these go well, other opportunities come—in college, in church work, in the military, on a job, in other adult settings. Future leaders gradually ascend a leadership ladder with increasingly important jobs, more challenging assignments, larger spans of control, more people to supervise, larger budgets, more complex issues, more power.

Some organizations deliberately foster these spirals. In the U.S. Army, a young officer—at age 21-25—will first command a platoon of thirty to fifty soldiers, next—at age 25-35—a company of perhaps 250 soldiers, third—age 35-45—a battalion of 1,000 soldiers, working ever higher through division, armies, theaters, containing thousands of troops, commanded by those in their 40s and 50s who have been promoted to the rank of general officer, with one to four stars on their shirt collars. In the Army, it would be unthinkable to put people in charge of larger units if they had no experience directing smaller ones; the earlier experience is considered absolutely crucial.

The same is true in most other organizations, though career progressions may not be as neatly organized. Gradual advancement builds the skills and self-confidence a leader needs to take on larger challenges and broader responsibilities.

Their willingness, even eagerness to accept responsibility has a direct influence on the careers of leaders; they tend to migrate into that part of the working environment where "leadership" is going on. They are seldom found in back offices, tucked away in libraries, or hidden in research labs. They like line or command positions; whether things are going well or poorly, they want to be in the chain of action.

This is a curious point, worth expanding on. Within a typical pyramidal organization—broad at the base with lots of workers, narrow at the top with only a few leaders—leaders can be found at all levels. They usually play three roles simultaneously:

Leader—supervising their subordinates,
Follower—being supervised by those at a higher level, and
Peer—working side by side with people of equal rank.

Good leaders are usually willing to play all three

roles; not only are they good leaders, but they tend to make good peers and good followers as well.

There are exceptions, especially entrepreneurial leaders, those creative, restless people who start new endeavors and run them mainly as loners. Still, a willingness to work within a chain of action setting is definitely characteristic of most people who make it to the top.

Leaders Are Good at Whatever They Are "Leadering In"

They have to be, or they can't gain and hold the support of their followers.

The athletic team captain is usually one of the best athletes on the team.

The "surgeon-in-charge" is usually the most skillful member of the operating team.

The head of the mountaineering expedition has spent more time on 5.11 walls (the very steep ones) than any of the other teammates.

Under such conditions, skill or knowledge creates the leadership power. If you wish to gain and hold leadership responsibility, you must constantly practice your task-relevant skills. (Sounds like the punch line to a bad joke. "What do you want to do tonight dear?" "Well, I think I'll practice my task-relevant skills.")

This generalization also has exceptions, and these can be troublesome. In many organizations, there is constant pressure to promote people who excel in the group's specialty. The best scientist is appointed project leader, the best teacher is advanced to principal, the best salesperson is promoted to sales manager, then, sometimes, trouble starts. The fact that they are good at selling, outstanding in the lab, or effective as teachers is no guarantee that they will succeed as administrators. Generally, new leaders need a transition period to learn the necessary administrative skills. Fortunately, most of them eventually do.

A leader must get things done, which means organizing others, setting goals, establishing procedures, monitoring progress, straightening out snarls, rewarding accomplishments, and preventing the recurrence of failures. These are administrative skills, and they are probably the easiest part of the leader's job to learn through formal instruction. Most leadership training programs or management development seminars focus on administration, and such training can be valuable.

A subcomponent of these administrative skills is the ability to gather outside resources, and this can be a major determinant of the leader's ability to attract followers. Leaders who can go out into the world and bring back the bacon are the ones that followers stick with. Politicians who win elections, athletes who win games, scientists who attract research funds, executives who raise capital or improve profits, union leaders who earn concessions from the company, network executives who can raise the program ratings—these are the people that find themselves out in front.

Sometimes leaders are lucky and the resources fall into their laps. More often it is not luck; they are simply more knowledgeable than others about where the gold is buried. "Dig here," says the leader, "you will find riches." The people dig; if the resources are there, the leader's power is strengthened. If not, well, the people may give the leader another chance or two, but three consecutive barren holes is probably the maximum. If you wish to evolve into a powerful leader, you had better spend some early years studying the treasure maps. One way to do it is to go out after dark, dig a few holes on your own, and see what you uncover.

Leaders can also put others at ease, negotiate disputes, communicate subtleties; many seem to have an instinctive feel for the emotions of others. These are only tendencies, of course, and not absolutes. Some leaders appear almost cruelly insensitive, but they are the exceptions, and in the long run they usually get what they deserve, good and hard. Most people in leadership positions are socially skillful—they should be, they get a lot of practice.

Leaders Are Energetic

Leadership requires energy. The hours are long, the pace is fast, the demands are multiple. Deadlines swarm over you, all sorts of people want a piece of your time, materials must be read, budgets reviewed, achievers celebrated, visitors welcomed, subordinates counseled—the list spins on endlessly. It is important to be healthy, durable, able to endure hardships, handle stress, and rebound from setbacks.

"There were days, in the spring and summer of 1973, when I fell into bed at two in the morning and lay there, telling myself that I was crazy. At seventy-five I was working longer hours than I had ever worked before and traveling more, both inside Israel and abroad, than was good for anyone. Although I really did my best to cut down on appointments and delegate more work, it was much too late for me to turn into another person. . . . There was only one way I could be prime minister and that was by talking to the people who wanted to talk to me and listening to the people who had something to tell me."
Golda Meir
My Life
G. P. Putnam's Sons

Further, leaders usually have some strong sense of physical dominance about them. They may be tall and handsome; they may be huge, with craggy faces; they may be astonishingly beautiful. They may be short and wiry with a coiled-spring feeling of physical tension about them. They may have strong, booming baritone voices or a penetrating, shrill, reedy quality to their speech. There is usually some physically arresting quality about them that conveys the sense that they are unusual people.

Leaders Are Good Communicators

Good leaders tend to be good speakers, good writers, and good conversationalists. So much of leadership consists of informing and persuading others that someone who cannot communicate cannot succeed.

Many times, communication is merely a matter of building image. A politician who can communicate trust and integrity, a corporation president who can communicate self-confident competence, an orchestra conductor who can communicate talented charisma—these are the people we follow. Communication is more than speaking and writing; all sorts of other factors are involved—body language, type of dress, location where the exchange occurs. The good leader is sensitive to many different communication channels.

The two basic communication skills—speaking and writing—are central, and they are skills you can practice and continue to develop over your entire career. The younger you begin, the better, but no matter what your age you can always improve.

One of the best techniques for improvement—and one which surprisingly few people use—is to watch other people who are good and model yourself after them.

There are many good writers around. Read them, notice how they do it, pay attention to their specific techniques, copy their approaches, and then practice. The way to learn to write is to write and write and write, and then to edit your words ruthlessly.

Good speakers are even more common than good writers. Watch them, study them. How do they do it? What words do they use? What expressions? What body language? What techniques? Exactly what do poor speakers do that bothers you? Study them also, and avoid their mistakes. Good speaking is something you can practice continuously; you do it every day.

If you can write and speak clearly, you have half the leadership game won.

Sense of Humor

Although I know of no study that supports this contention, I am convinced that a majority of good leaders have an above-average sense of humor. They are cheerful, jovial, filled with jokes, quotes, and anecdotes. Making light of life helps them to survive the pressure of the leadership role.

Humor is an enormous asset. Much of a leader's life is spent in repetitious drudgery—staff meetings, budget development, routine personnel matters. Other activities occur in psychologically abrasive settings—negotiations, confrontations, conflicts, competitions. Anger and hostility are present, tempers flare, sharp words are thrown. In such situations, the release created by humor can be invaluable. If you don't have a well-developed sense of humor, I, for one, hope I never have to follow you.

John Kennedy was a national leader with far more than his share of humor; he had a whimsical grace about him that enchanted the country during his brief period of national visibility.

"[An example of the Kennedy humor] involved crowd estimates, always a bone of contention between the press and the presidential candidate. Once the Kennedy apparatus had announced that a JFK rally had been attended by 35,000 people, a figure which seemed to the traveling reporters to be substantially high. I asked Kennedy how they had arrived at this figure, and he said to me and half a dozen other reporters: "Plucky (press secretary Pierre Salinger's nickname) counts the nuns and then multiplies by 100." By so deprecating the crowd count, and making a joke about a subject that was sensitive, to say the least, Kennedy made the reporters laugh, and probably avoided a story about inflated crowd counts by his staff."

Benjamin Bradlee
Conversations with Kennedy
W. W. Norton & Co.

In summary, psychological studies of leaders suggest that they are bright, skillful, energetic, effective communicators who seek out responsibility. But the studies also suggest that the differences between leaders and non-leaders are not large; many times, the situational differences are at least as important as personal differences in determining who has what power and who gets what done.

To understand that, we must look more closely at the leadership environment and the forces operating there.

III

What Is Leadership?

Leadership is any *action* that focuses *resources* to create *new opportunities.*

Action. Leadership is active, not passive. It may be mental—as in the development of a new philosophy—but even then nothing much happens unless the philosophy is written down or explained in speeches; brilliant thoughts are not sufficient. Generally, leaders are in motion—in meetings, on airplanes, touring facilities, campaigning door-to-door, negotiating, planning, talking, creating—the most frequent emphasis is on action.

Resources. The resources to be focused should be broadly conceived: time, energy, people, money, talent, public opinion, physical facilities, new laws, anything a leader can use to make new things happen.

New Opportunities. These can cover a wide range, including items such as new jobs, higher profits, better entertainment, improved health, travel, happiness, education, expanded individual options, love, wealth, long life.

Sometimes leadership may be only the creation of an image—if people *think* opportunities are increasing, even in the absence of actual change, opportunities will probably grow more numerous. If the world appears better today than it did yesterday, a leader may have succeeded without changing anything "real." Morale is mainly a reflection of how people perceive their world. If a leader can improve that perception, thereby improving morale, more energy and enthusiasm will result, new things will happen, new opportunities will be created, and the leadership can be judged successful.

This analysis reduces reality to simple, clean concepts. In contrast, real leaders—people in charge—exist in a turbulent, churning whirlpool where each day is a problem of keeping one's head above water, where forward progress is often impossible to detect, where issues of morale, perception, and opportunities can get lost in the pressure of deadlines, meetings, budgets, grievances, and brush fires. To avoid being at the mercy of the current, the leader must find some patterns in this turbulence that can be used to create effective action. So next we turn to what leaders actually do, and look for some patterns there.

The following was prepared by Jane Gorrell, an 18-year-old retiring yearbook editor, for the benefit of her successor, Drew Campbell. The issues referred to are universal.

THE EDITOR'S OATH

I promise not to let the enthusiasm and creativity of the summer dwindle, especially when laying out mug shots.

I promise to keep the peace with subordinates and listen to each dumbass idea with the same eagerness I would my own great ideas.

I promise to be patient with colleagues— even when they decide to ride their own horses.

I vow to be organized.

I promise not to throw temper tantrums due to stress (especially like slamming doors and crying in the bathroom).

I will strive to be a strong leader, but not a dictator.

I will not hesitate to ask others before me for advice; too much pride can screw up a deadline.

I promise not to spend all my money and be in the red when bills need to be paid.

I promise to be superhuman.

IV

What Do Leaders Do?

If you are a leader, you will find a wide range of obligations competing for your attention on any given day. Here is a typical agenda.

LIST TO DO TODAY

1) Plan the agenda for the group meeting next week, reviewing progress to date.
2) Decide how to intercede between two subordinates who are clashing over whose turf is whose.
3) Send a small gift to a colleague who stepped in last week to help you out of a personal jam.
4) Get some pictures taken to document one of your recent successes.
5) Figure out how to warn the business office that you may go over budget next month.
6) Read the new bulletin that just came in with information affecting your freedom in making personnel decisions.
7) Meet with three or four of your workers who are trying to get the kinks out of a new process.
8) Review a technical article describing a combination TV/recorder/camera system that seems perfect for your communication needs, and figure out how to justify the cost.

9) Get a card in the mail to your mother, remembering her birthday.

10) Survey materials from your competitors to look for new ideas.

11) Write a short speech you have been asked to give at a luncheon, honoring a colleague whose achievements you admire but whose personality is too abrasive for your taste.

12) Transfer some money from your savings account to your checking account to cover the big check you just mailed.

13) Figure out how to recruit the talented young person you met last week at an evening meeting.

14) Set up an appointment with the person responsible for your advertising budget to plan a strategy for using those funds.

15) Fill in a registration form for a two-day seminar on a new technology, and figure out how to fit those two days into your schedule.

16) Return a phone call to someone who has offered you a new opportunity, but first think at some length about how it might fit into your own career progression.

17) Review the snafu that occurred in last week's schedule when six people were given the wrong assignments, and figure out how to prevent its recurrence.

18) Develop a strategy for dealing with a colleague who has taken on new responsibilities far beyond his ability and is now fouling up everything, some of which affects you and your operation.

19) Call a friend to schedule a racquetball game.

20) Find time to wander around and chat with a few members of your organization informally, just to keep a finger on the pulse of what is happening.

Scanning this list leads to some immediate conclusions.

First, *there is no way that all of those items are* **EVER** *going to be covered, let alone today.* Progress can be made, but in most leadership positions, the number of new daily additions to your list exceeds the number eliminated yesterday. The longer you are in a leadership position, the more unattended loose ends you will have flapping in the breeze.

Second, *the nature of these daily activities does not change markedly as one climbs the ladder of power.* The above list is just as appropriate for the editor of a high school yearbook as it is for a state governor, a professional football coach, or a corporation president. The stakes are higher in the latter cases, and the impacts greater, but the complexities are similar, and the relentlessness of competing deadlines is identical. This similarity of process over many levels is one reason why early experience in leadership roles is so helpful.

Third, *in this listing of daily activities, there is no single unifying theme,* nor even any obvious ordering of priorities. Many managers yearn for a crystal ball that will tell them what is important, what is crucial, and what is trivial. Many management techniques have been developed to serve this need for focus. "Goal Setting," "Annual Plans," and "Management by Objectives" are some of the techniques used to create order in the daily chaos, and research data support the

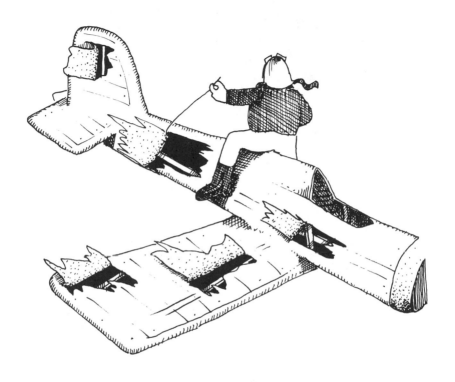

notion that this focus is necessary in most organizations. Someone has to say, "This is what we believe in, this is the path we are following, other activities are diversions." Otherwise, competing loose ends can tie an organization in knots. Priorities are important, even though they sometimes feel arbitrary. Who is to say that it is really more important to work on next year's budget than it is to send a birthday card to your mother, especially if she votes some of the corporate stock?

Fourth, *there is little danger of being bored in a leadership position.* One of the most delicious aspects of being in charge is the range of daily activities. You may be harried, hassled, or frustrated, but you will never be bored. When you are in command, your world has a momentum that makes the hours whistle by.

"The forty hour week has no charm for me.
I'm looking for a forty hour day."
Dr. Nicholas Murray Butler
President, Columbia University

One of the real dangers in a leadership role is that there are so many interesting things to do that necessary but dreary portions of the job may be slighted. The drudgery of management—periodic reports, contract minutiae, routine follow-ups, staff planning sessions, distasteful personnel actions—are ignored in favor of the fun stuff—action projects, interesting people, travel, social events, and figure-head occasions where the leader is visible out front. Because leadership is usually synonymous with action, those attracted to leadership roles are action-oriented, and as soon as they start feeling bland about the day's routine, they organize a new project.

How can we organize leadership activities so that we can understand them better? One way is by looking at the areas that anyone in charge has to deal with.

- Day-to-day operations
- Finances
- The future

- Membership renewal
- Telling your story
- Protecting your turf
- Tradition and rituals
- Your own career
- Your personal life

Day-to-Day Operations

In most organizations there is a day-to-day momentum that keeps the operation going. If you are running a small manufacturing plant, materials come in the front door, orders come in through the mail, and the finished product goes out by way of the loading dock. To stay in business, you must see that this system operates efficiently every day, and problems related to these operations must be given first priority. If you are a school principal, students show up every day and the classroom schedule maintains the pace. If you are a newspaper editor, there is the unceasing demand of deadlines. Even in organizations like universities or research laboratories where the pace is less structured, the momentum of daily activities is almost irresistible. When scientists from research labs or universities are given a year's sabbatical leave with complete freedom to do what they want, they invariably comment on the difficulty of adjusting to a schedule with no routine inertia in it.

This part of a leader's daily life might be characterized more as "management" than "leadership." It is usually a matter of assigning priorities, delegating responsibility and authority, setting up systems to monitor progress, anticipating crises and trying to avert them before they arise—in short, keeping the ship afloat, well-painted, and pointed in the right direction.

More energy is required to maintain this routine in organizations without a fixed product, such as volunteer one-meeting-a-month groups. Because there is no daily momentum, more leadership imagination has to be devoted to keeping the organization on track and motivated.

Finances

A concern for finances pervades an organization's activities and provides the most direct, immediate constraint on what the leader can do. If you are president of the local square dancing association, your budget is going to determine how often the newsletter goes out, the quality of the band that you can hire for monthly dances, and whether your organization can afford to send you, its representative, to the National Square Dancing Convention. If you are commander of a National Guard battalion, finances will determine whether you have enough ammo to practice live firing or must resort to simulated types of training. If you are president of a computer leasing company, the flow of money between you, your customers, and your financing institutions may be the most important

factor in your success, curiously, even more important than the quality of computer that you build.

You might be president, commander, director, or even the risk-taker that founded your organization, without understanding the specifics of its cash position. There are thousands of people in such positions right now who are ignorant of finances; it is not a lethal defect. Still, if you don't understand your organization's financing, you are vulnerable in an important area. If you aspire to higher levels of leadership, you should have some accounting in your background so, at the minimum, you can understand the financial restraints upon your operation.

A reverse danger—I have seen it often—lies in the possibility that once people in power understand finances, they become fixated on dollars to the exclusion of other equally important but less quantifiable considerations. You won't be intimidated by such people if you understand your organization's accounting systems; this is a good reason to learn.

The Future

While the momentum of the ongoing schedule is a sign of progress in the management of day-to-day activities, planning for the future may be handicapped by this same momentum. Unless you abandon yourself to daily demands and allow them to force your future upon you, future planning probably implies a change in direction. Because changing directions makes most people nervous, planning for the future is sometimes scary. A personal philosophy of life that favors change is useful here, and the best future planning is typically done by people who are innovative, willing to experiment and, if necessary, to pay the price of some inevitable failures. Aspiring leaders who wish to control their own futures need to develop these risk-taking propensities; otherwise a stagnant status quo may reign and moss will grow.

Membership Renewal

If you are in an organization with a high turnover of membership, such as a special interest group or a political party, your abiding concern will be the addition of new members. As people lose interest and drop out, you must maintain the flow of new membership, which means making certain that your organization is attractive to the kind of people you wish to recruit, and that they know about you. Without such efforts, your organization will die.

In organizations where the membership is stable and the same people are around for several years—government agencies, stable trade organizations, family businesses, university departments—your major problem in this area will be renewal. This means structuring your environment so that the people in it are stimulated to learn new skills, take on new responsibilities, and avoid stagnation.

"Good leaders are those who are constantly rear-ranging their world so that they and their people can continually learn from it. "
David DeVries
Director of Research
Center for Creative
Leadership

Telling Your Story

As the leader of any organization, you will continually find it necessary to tell your story: selling your group's talents to prospective members or customers, explaining your programs to clients, documenting your actions to various publics, establishing the value of your activities to crucial legislative bodies. Whether you are running a soccer program and you want the park department's continued financing, arguing for more liberal export regulations for your trade association, or managing a paper mill making new kinds of paper for the printing industry, you want the people who are going to make decisions about your operation to know who you are and what you have been accomplishing.

The techniques for getting your story out will be mulled over incessantly—"Shall we write a letter, take out an ad, commission a movie, use four-color prints in our annual report, convene a conference, run a telephone campaign, buy a TV spot, put out a mass mailing, or use a billboard?" Every organization deals with these issues constantly.

If you are an apprentice leader, still young and learning in a leadership position at a modest level, you should experiment with as many ways of getting your story out as possible. Controlling the flow of information is central to all leadership positions, and the better you understand the specific techniques, the more successful you will be. While you are young, start practicing. Write ads, lay out brochures, get yourself on TV talk shows, design posters. Some day, in ways you cannot now predict, the experience will prove useful.

Protecting Your Turf

All organizations and their leaders are affected by decisions made outside of their boundaries. The university coach finds that the procedures for recruiting new athletes are determined by NCAA decisions. The company architect finds that new building designs are restricted to those acceptable to the family of the Chief Executive Officer. The president of a state professional organization realizes that the state licensing board determines who can belong to the group.

There is usually nothing malicious or hostile about this external control. It is simply a fact of life; no leader is powerful enough to control everything. External pressures do exist, and the best leader may be the one who carefully anticipates and guides them.

Frequently it is merely a matter of information flow. If the outside decision-makers are kept informed about what you are doing and why it is important, they may be cooperative in helping you. If you are constantly surprising them, straining their system, and creating embarrassment, you will often find yourself feeling beleaguered by their demands.

Probably the best strategy for protecting your turf against outsiders is to cultivate friendships in their camp. In the political arena, one common technique for doing this is lobbying. An organization hires a professional "friend," a lobbyist, to represent its interests to legislative bodies. The lobbyist is expected to keep the organization informed about developments that will affect it, and to represent it in any related legislative action.

Informal lobbying operations are usually found on the boundaries of most organizations. The physician who goes to lunch with the hospital administrator, the tavern owner who chats with the city planner at the annual St. Patrick's Day Green Beer Open House, the newspaper editor who plays golf with a major advertiser—all of them are protecting their turf, because the best protection in the long run is probably a trustworthy circle of friends and acquaintances who are as aware of the pressures on you as you are of the pressures on them. Mutual backscratching comes in many guises, and provides a useful lubrication for organizational activities.

Leaders who do not like these extroverted, social activities had better make certain that they have someone in their organization who does, and they had better not look too closely at those expense accounts. As the economist John Kenneth Galbraith said, with tongue in cheek, to be sure, "I continue to believe that bribery is the basis of most friendships." At the very least, to have friends you must spend time, the most irreplaceable of all your assets.

A second and important point in protecting your turf is that, along with building friendships, you must be careful not to create enemies. One active enemy can consume more of your psychological energy than is produced by several friends. Even more importantly, as someone once quipped, "Friends come and go, but enemies accumulate."

Keep your temper, say only those things about others that you can easily say to their faces, and remember that when people do nasty, unwarranted things to you, there may be something unrelated going on in their lives that affects the way they are treating you. Stay calm. A charitable approach protects a lot of turf.

Traditions and Rituals

Every organization has its rituals and traditions to which the leader must attend. The range is great. At one extreme, if you have formed a neighborhood group to keep a freeway out of your front yard, there will be few traditions and little ritualistic behavior. At the other extreme, if you are a pastor in charge of a church congregation, much of your time will be devoted to traditional rituals: weddings, baptisms, funerals, and other events that mark important changes in people's lives. Every collection of people recognizes some rites of passage, and at Christmas parties, going-away parties, showers for new babies, or summer picnics, the leader usually plays a figurehead role.

Rituals serve useful functions: they act as a cohesive glue, giving expression to common beliefs and purposes; they provide a source of stability by marking calendar events; they provide mileposts in our lives by setting aside note-worthy occasions and highlighting special accomplishments.

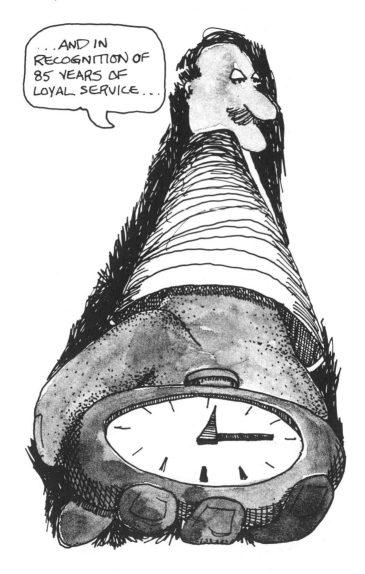

A leader who ignores or impedes organizational rituals as "frivolous," or "not cost-effective," is ignoring the rhythms of history and our collective conditioning. Rituals are the punctuation marks that make sense out of the passage of time; without them, there are no beginnings and no endings. Life becomes an endless series of Wednesdays.

The Leader's Own Career

Leaders must constantly be aware of what is happening to them in terms of their own careers. Even the President of the United States, usually considered the most powerful person on earth, is always concerned with his career progression, especially with the next election. Leadership savvy, wonderful principles, and talented staff are worth nothing if an election goes to the other side. This example illustrates the principle more clearly than most—unemployed leaders don't have much fun.

The Leader's Personal Life

Equally obvious but not well attended to by some people in planning their careers is the impact of family situations on their effectiveness as leaders. In situation after situation, the one thing that will break an important leader out of a tight schedule is a family consideration such as a sick spouse, a graduation ceremony, or a child in trouble.

I once had an hour's appointment with a university president concerning a topic near and dear to my heart—my own career—when a phone call came from his insurance agent concerning the sports car his son had wrapped around a telephone pole the night before. With considerable amusement, I listened to his end of the conversation, watching this powerful man, truly an intellectual giant, grapple with his confused feelings—confused because the son had not been hurt but the car had been damaged beyond repair. He ran through the entire gamut of parental emotions, from deep relief at his son's safety to extreme irritation that the episode was going to cost him several thousand dollars.

Such episodes do not appear on anyone's job description, yet they require attention and, indeed, are central to life. The importance of friends and family can hardly be exaggerated. A common feeling among older people looking back over their lives is that friendship and love were to be valued above all else.

> "If asked which has given me most pleasure in my life, art, writing, or friendship, I think I would answer friendship. (A rare value) is a friend whom I have known for almost 60 years and to whom I can say anything."
>
> Kenneth Clark
> Eminent British Writer
> in his autobiography,
> The Other Half
> Harper and Row, 1978

These, then, are the nine areas that all leaders must deal with simultaneously:

1. Day-to-day operations
2. Finances
3. The future
4. Membership renewal
5. Telling their stories
6. Protecting their turf
7. Traditions and rituals
8. Their own careers
9. Their personal lives

No wonder life seems so complex.

How do leaders do it? The next chapter organizes these areas into the various roles that leaders play.

V

The Roles
Leaders Play

To accomplish what they do, leaders must lead complex lives, playing different roles at different times for different purposes. Professor Henry Mintzberg of McGill University observed five Chief Executive Officers (CEOs), people at the top of major corporations, in his book, *The Nature of Managerial Work.* He spent a week with each of them and, from his observations, concluded that ten roles, grouped into three broad categories, are necessary to describe what people at the top do all day. People reaching for leadership positions should study these roles and the skills that each requires, and begin focusing on weaknesses they perceive in themselves.

Here is the Mintzberg listing:

• Interpersonal Roles
    Leader
    Liaison
    Figurehead

- Informational Roles
  - Monitor
  - Disseminator
  - Spokesperson
- Decision Roles
  - Entrepreneur
  - Resource Allocator
  - Disturbance Handler
  - Negotiator

Interpersonal Roles

In these roles, the emphasis is on relationships with others.

Leader—Motivating, directing, assigning tasks, assessing performance, inspiring by example, coaching, following up.

This is the role that most people think about when they think of leadership—the charisma, the sparkling eyes, the vibrant voice, the fire in one's belly. Most leadership training programs focus on this aspect, and more is probably known about this role than the others that a leader plays. Strangely, however, while it may be central in many leadership positions, this role is not necessarily crucial. If the person in charge is good in the remaining roles, and especially if the organization is structured so that organizational issues dominate, as in an entrenched bureaucracy or a tenured professional constituency, the pure "fire in the belly" leadership role may be less important. Certainly, there are many suc-

cessful organizations led by people who are hardly inspiring personal leaders.

"Life is a romantic business. It is painting a picture, not doing a sum; but you have to make the romance, and it will finally come to the question of how much fire you have in your belly."
Oliver Wendell Holmes

"I set myself on fire and people come to watch me burn."
John Wesley
Founder of Methodism

Liaison—Dealing with interested outsiders, communicating with peers on your own level, making contacts, scouting for new resources, playing politics.

"There are three ways to get to the top of an oak tree:
1. Climb it.
2. Sit on an acorn.
3. Make friends with a very big bird."

Leaders in all organizations interact with others over whom they have no control. These interactions, which cannot be considered "leadership" in the usual sense because no power is exercised, still might be more influential than anything else a leader does for the future of an organization. Problems can be identified and headed off, new resources can be developed, new allies can be found. The high school newspaper editor who finds a cheap, used typewriter while talking to a fellow editor at a sports car rally, the corporate V.P. who stumbles onto a new sales contact while visiting an old college friend in a strange city, a university department chairperson who finds a new funding source while talking with a professional colleague in a bar at a national convention are engaging in liaison activities—no power is directly involved, no decisions, no planning, just alertness and a large collection of well-placed acquaintances.

In my position as Vice-President of the Center for Creative Leadership I have sat in on many conversations, both in our institution and in many others, where the hiring of new, high-level people was being discussed. Inevitably, questions arose about the prospect's contacts:

> *"Does this person know the corporate world?" (Implication: Does he or she have a long list of acquaintances in appropriate places who will provide needed entry?)*

> *"Is the individual familiar with Washington?" (Implication: If we have a specific question, does this person know who to go to for an answer?)*

> *"Is this person well-connected in the black community or the women's movement or with labor unions?" (Implication: Those are separate cultures and we need some credible go-between to get anything done.)*

It usually comes down to whether the people under consideration have been engaged in liaison activities before or whether they, like most of us, are recluses in their own organizations and industries. There are surprisingly few people who play the liaison role well.

The best liaison people need not be good leaders themselves. The classic strong leaders are frequently too independent and too busy to spend much time building connections outside of their own institutions; because of the press of business, they tend to be homebodies. Consequently, many leaders need to surround themselves with others who enjoy the vague, ambiguous liaison activities, and then listen to them.

Figurehead—Appearing at formal and informal functions, passing out contest trophies, welcoming dignitaries from other organizations, commenting on new babies, and announcing promotions and new contracts; ceremonial, social, and highly visible.

Curiously, although this is an important and visible part of the leader's job, people promoted into positions of leadership are seldom trained in these skills; no one is ever taught how to award the gold watch, to welcome the winning sports team home from the state tournament, to greet the astronauts returning from the moon. Like some other skills, leaders probably learn this one from watching other leaders on television.

People who are good in the ceremonial role usually have a collection of stories, jokes, and quotes useful for all occasions (or a staff member who is good at finding them) and have practiced their "adlibs" the night before.

Having a leader who performs well in the figurehead role can bestow a feeling of warmth, style, and stability on an organization. During my early career as a faculty member at the university of Minnesota, the University was led by President O. Meredith Wilson. A scholar with a sense of humor and power about him, he could always be counted on for a short statement, with both noble and humorous quotes, at faculty gatherings, student retreats, and commencements. Although I had virtually no other data to judge the man from, his performance in these public settings, where some fleeting sense of his character was visible, led me to have faith that all was going well in the Presidential Suite. I cannot now, many years later, remember a single Wilson quote, but another university president has been credited with a fine example:

> *"The faculty consists of a group of dedicated professionals held together by a common concern—finding a place to park."*
> Clark Kerr, President
> University of California

Informational Roles

Knowledge is power and the leader plays several roles that reflect this truism.

Monitor—Reading, listening, looking through statistical tables, studying journals, attending workshops, walking through convention displays, taking tours through your own facilities.

The effective leader continually scans the horizon for information: written, oral, visual, political, and personal, inside and outside the organization. It may come from newspapers, staff reports, the casual comments of customers, workers, clients, or colleagues, or from any of the several dozen sources with which a normal leader intersects in a typical week. Useful, important facts and leads must be sifted out and acted upon; the trivia must be ignored.

Some managers are superb at setting up informational systems to improve their monitoring skills. This is worth the effort, since most leaders suffer from information overload. More information is available than they can attend to, and methods to condense and highlight important trends are useful.

You should monitor a wide range of input and

be particularly careful that no censoring, deliberate or otherwise, is going on. Some leaders build walls around themselves to screen out unpleasant information and feel surprised when the rug is jerked out from under them. One way to avoid unpleasant surprises is to spend some time regularly with the people in your organization who actually do the work—the factory workers, the troops, the writers, the cooks, the students—whoever is on the front line. Many top people remove themselves from the core of their organization and find out too late that some of it is rotten. Stay in touch; you'll learn a lot.

Disseminator—Speaking, writing, informing, sharing, distributing.

Once the information has been monitored, the leader must decide which pieces should be passed along, and to whom. A good disseminator has several systems working: staff meetings, memos, informal briefing sessions, weekly letters, bulletin boards, luncheon meetings, perhaps even closed circuit television or videotapes. A common complaint in many organizations is that "no one ever tells me what is going on around here," and the good leader tries to prevent this by keeping everyone informed.

Information is a form of power in itself because the information disseminated tells members what is important. If cost figures are shared and stressed, people will be cost-conscious. If a timetable is stressed, schedules will be paramount. If TV ratings are distributed, audience size will be considered important. The index highlighted in the daily (weekly, monthly, annual) report will take on extra meaning, and the organization will gear itself up to improve in this area. The mere collection and sharing of information creates a focus that is influential.

Spokesperson—Selling, informing, taking a

stand, making contacts, representing your people to the world.

All organizations need representation to the outside world; someone must speak for them. The Pep Club needs a voice on the Student Council so that rallies will be scheduled at the right time; corporation management must be represented to the stockholders; the orchestra must be represented in the Arts Council so that its fund-raising drive will be properly handled.

The role of spokesperson is best played by someone who is fluent and well-prepared. The role can be formal, complete with rehearsed speech and overhead transparencies. More often, a leader will assume the role of spokesperson in informal settings—at picnics and cocktail parties, at committee meetings and tennis matches, at dances and athletic contests and shopping malls and neighborhood barbecues. Anyone playing the spokesperson's role for an organization will find many informal opportunities to catch the ear of someone who needs to be informed; consequently, leaders should always be prepared with relevant facts.

"The new uniforms are going to cost us $30.00 more; as I remember, we put some money into a contingency fund for this."

"This year the university saved the taxpayers an estimated $5 million through an improved program of wheat rust control."

"Our company has created 56 new jobs for the hard-core unemployed."

"Our Chamber spearheaded the program that brought 200 families back into the center city."

Decision Roles

In these roles, choices have to be made, crises quelled, resources must be allocated, and competing viewpoints resolved.

Entrepreneur—Seeking opportunities, taking chances, trying new things, assuming risks.

The entrepreneurial leader is always looking for the vein of gold—seeking new products, exploring new territories, prospecting. This is a risky but necessary part of the leader's job; to keep an organization alive, thriving, and growing, someone must continually find new resources and new ways to use the organization's resources. Because these are new activities, there is always an element of risk involved.

In the entrepreneurial role, the leader must play internal hunches. There is never enough solid data to prove that a risky course of action is justified. Many times, the entrepreneur identifies an opportunity and takes action "just because it feels right."

The entrepreneurial role is one in which you are usually leading with your chin—putting your ideas up front where others can swing at them.

Your success will depend both on how good your judgement is and on how much glass you have in your jaw, for you will continually hear reactions to your plans like these:

"Frisbee, what's a frisbee—it'll never fly."

"Jaws, what a stupid name for a movie."

"Edsel, gee, Mr. Ford, that name has a nice ring to it."

"Raise our prices ten percent, I wonder . . . ?"

"Lower our prices ten percent, well, how do we know . . . ?"

"Commission a sculpture for the City Center that looks like a schizophrenic poodle?!"

"You're going after this nomination by walking across the state of Illinois; you gotta be crazy."

But while entrepreneurs suffer sweaty palms and uneasy stomachs, the jubilation surrounding the occasional success makes it worthwhile. Undoubtedly there are people somewhere right now sitting around, thinking:

"I wonder if people would buy a chewing gum that turned different colors at different body temperatures; they could even throw away their thermometers."

"What this sales agency needs is a full-time hypnotist."

"We could start a Dial-A-Reunion service; someone could call us, tell us what they want, and we'd call their aunts and uncles and get something going."

Charles F. Kettering, the great inventive genius of General Motors, once said:

> "Whenever you look at a piece of work and you think the fellow was crazy, then you want to pay some attention to that. One of you is likely to be, and you had better find out which. It makes an awful lot of difference."

Almost 500 years ago, a now famous Italian engineer described the plight of the innovator:

> ". . . there is nothing more difficult to plan, more doubtful of success, nor more dangerous to manage than the creation of a new system. For the innovator has the enmity of all who would profit by the preservation of the old institutions and merely lukewarm defenders in those who would gain by the new ones. The hesitation of the latter arises in part from the fear of their adversaries, who have current laws on their side, and in part from the general skepticism of mankind which does not really believe in an innovation until experience proves its value. So it happens that whenever his enemies have occasion to attack the innovator, they do so with the passion of partisans while his supporters defend him sluggishly, so that both the innovator and his party are vulnerable."
>
> Niccolo Machiavelli
> *The Prince,* 1513

Resource Allocator—Budgeting, deciding who gets what, assigning priorities, giving out dollars, time, and space.

Every organization has resources, and decisions about how to distribute them are made at the top. Financial resources, the cash, are usually allocated through the budgeting process, and this is one of the most important features of the leader's job; recognizing this, most take an active role in financial planning. But leaders control other resources also.

The commander of the State Highway Patrol can decide what percentage of patrol cars to assign to city freeway duty and what percentage to more leisurely outstate, rural patrolling. (The former is more publicly visible, the latter is more favored by the patrol officers.)

The head of a research lab controls not only the budget but also the allotment of laboratory and office space.

The head of a political campaign—the candidate—can decide how campaign time will be used, what hoopla will be featured.

Directors of performing organizations— bands, orchestras, dance troupes, repertory casts—can determine how their most important resource—practice time—should be spent.

Allocation of resources is probably the *least appreciated, least understood, yet most important* component of leadership.

It is *most important* because most influential leadership decisions must be handled far upstream of their actual occurrence—months or even years ahead of the actual event. You cannot decide overnight to drastically change the course of your organization and expect to see it happen the following day. Plans must be made, budgets must be established, advertising must be prepared, notifications must be made, patents must be secured, people must be hired—and all of this must happen as a result of earlier allocation decisions. Allocation is the magic wand.

It is *least understood* because precise studies of how organizations allocate their resources and the resulting impact of these allocations have not been done, and may be almost impossible to do. Leaders have to learn through their own experiences, in favored apprentice roles, or they must trust their instincts. The amount of advertising purchased, the dollars spent on research, the time and energy devoted to public relations, office decoration, public service, or employee training programs—these are all allocation decisions and they are all made basically by instinct and experience.

When people talk about "vision" on the part of a leader, they are usually referring to allocation decisions. The leader with vision funds the solar energy system that won't be in place for five years, purchases exotic computer equipment without really knowing its capacity, opens a foreign branch without truly understanding the new culture, opens a retail outlet in an untested area, spends the candidate's time on a unique media blitz, requires schools to bus children for racial integration. These are all leadership decisions with long lead times involving the allocation of resources; each is saturated with uncertainty, can have great eventual impact, and is based on faith as much as hard data. Leaders with accurate hunches ("vision") stay on, the others move on.

The allocation role is *least appreciated* because allocation decisions are seldom made in ways that are visible to the people involved. A Chief Executive Officer may decide that the corporation needs a new research lab, ramrod it through the management committee, sell it to the Board of Directors, oversee initial construction, and yet be long gone before the lab is flourishing. The people who benefit most, the research scientists with their up-to-date equipment and unfettered inquiry time, may have little appreciation of who made the decision and at what psychological cost their facility was built; the leader with the vision that improved their world won't even be known to them. Indeed, instead of feeling grateful for their new toys, they will probably moan and groan because there are not enough gas taps, too little storage space, or insufficient parking. Allocation decisions have to be made so far ahead of the actual event that those affected are seldom aware of the vision involved or of the personal battles fought by the leader in fending off other demands on the money.

It is this feature of leadership—long-range vision in allocating resources—that creates much of the "loneliness at the top." Because resources may have to be taken away from existing personnel, leaving them feeling wounded and unwanted, and given to others not yet around to provide support, the leader's life can be lonely. The wounded and unwanted don't make good tennis partners, and the newly supported aren't on the scene yet. It is not future decisions, but the futurity of current decisions that eats away at the leader's self-assurance.

Disturbance Handler—Reacting to crises, putting out fires, soothing ruffled feathers, calming and solving through decisive action.

"On any given day, somewhere in the world, there is probably a strike going on that falls within my area of responsibility."
Roger Kelley
Vice President, Personnel
Caterpillar Tractor Co.

This role is a waste of the leader's time, and whenever possible, good leaders organize it out of existence. If the right systems are in place, if the proper people have been trained, if the proper responsibility has been delegated, if the necessary equipment is available, if emergency drills have been practiced, if "rainy day" schedules have been prominently posted, if grievance and appeal procedures have been established and tested, if cash flow accounting procedures are well-developed, if checkpoints along the way to deadlines are met, the number of crises will be minimal.

But simply reading that list of "ifs" is revealing. They can't always be satisfied; crises will continue to occur. Still, excluding those working in true "catastrophe" environments—fire fighting, police work, military activities—if you are constantly rushing around quelling disturbances, you probably need to be better organized.

Negotiator—Bargaining with others, negotiating contracts, swapping resources, buying

time, straightening out errors, handling termina-
tions, cancellations, extra work, and failures.

Negotiating runs through a leader's life like
oxygen, vital to well-being but explosive in pure
concentrations.

Because negotiating is so central to the leadership role, and because some useful, highly
practical suggestions are available, I have in-
cluded a separate chapter on negotiating, which
follows next.

This chapter has listed the ten roles described
by Professor Mintzberg in his research on top
corporate leaders. They illustrate the reasons
why leadership positions are so complex; there
is no single, simple way to proceed. To be
effective, the leader needs to play many roles
simultaneously, and this variety is what keeps
many people in leadership positions. The daily
pace can be almost habit-forming.

VI

Negotiating: A Central Skill

Last year, at the invitation of Clay Hammer, a friend of mine at Duke University, I slipped into the back of his classroom to watch an invited lecturer address the class on Entrepreneurialism. He was Richard Hughes, a Yale-educated Okie from Tulsa who deals in venture capitalism—taking business risks with money. One of his major activities is buying and managing small companies, and he is continually in negotiations of one kind or another.

In his talk to these business school students, he emphasized that we live in a world of constant negotiations, whether these be with labor unions, clients, suppliers, bankers, superiors, subordinates, or family members. Hughes argued persuasively that not enough attention is paid to the role of negotiation in the affairs of the world, and that not enough people know how to do it well.

He was a thoughtful, fluent man with great stage presence and a pocketful of one-liners. ("The University is indeed the repository of the wisdom of the ages—the freshmen bring a lot in and the seniors don't take much out.")

Although his style was clearly that of a self-reliant loner who makes autocratic decisions, he was quite perceptive about the way the world is developing; when someone asked what he thought the management style of the future would be, he said, "consensus management," explaining that the best future managers would probably be those who can deal with a wide range of tensions.

Later, during the guest speaker reception, I asked him if he had any "commandments" on negotiations. He whipped off several:

1. **Do your research.** Always know what is going on; be better informed than the people with whom you are dealing.

2. **Recognize that people have egos.** Protect them. One way to do this is to provide visible, acceptable reasons for them to switch to your viewpoint.

3. **Try to understand what is important to the other side.** Sit down and roleplay your competition. Ask yourself what is paramount to them, and what it is they want from you.

4. **Determine what valuable services your competitors can offer you at no cost**

to themselves. Hughes cited his use of another company's research department as an example. "I'm not big enough to have a research department, but it doesn't cost a big corporation a thing to let me have access to some of their people to bounce questions off of."

5. **Keep the decision-makers out of the negotiating sessions.** Give yourself room to say, "I can't make that decision; I'll have to go home and check it with my Board." This gives you thinking time and keeps you from making commitments that look good in the heat of activity but less impressive when you get home. Hughes said, "I use my Board that way, even though I could make the decision. I say, 'I will have to check that one out at home.'"

6. **Never be afraid to walk away from a deal.** Never let yourself get into a situation where you think, "I have to close this one; it's the best opportunity I ever saw." He mused, "About 50 percent of the time, when you walk away from a deal that's not turning out the way you want it to, the other side will come after you later and you can go from there, probably in a stronger position."

Hughes's ideas, developed on the firing line, mesh nicely with a set of negotiating recommendations developed recently by Professor Robin

Williams, an eminent sociologist at Cornell University. Dr. Williams recently completed an extensive study of human conflict with a special focus on those situations which resulted in peaceful resolutions, that is, where negotiations were successful. In his book, *Mutual Accommodation: Ethnic Conflict and Cooperation* (University of Minnesota Press, 1978), he cites many tense cases in which riots *didn't* occur, strikes *were* averted, integration *wasn't* violent, and opposing viewpoints *were negotiated* into agreement. As a result of his intensive research, Williams offers the following suggestions to those who are involved in settling disputes:

1. **Keep all "weapons" out of reach.** Do not let the participants hurt each other. This may mean literally banning guns, knives, and fists, but it also means a ban on psychological weapons such as jeers, taunts, and threats.

2. **Avoid personalized attacks.** Use all of the social and psychological devices you know to keep negotiations free of highly personal topics, recriminations, abusive language, and especially those subtle jibes that people in conflict know so well how to inflict on each other. Humor is a great aid here.

3. **Find a "common coin."** Translate the issues into money or some other easily traded commodity. With "tradeable" items

to work with, agreements are easier to reach.

4. Fractionate the conflict. Break the BIG ISSUE into smaller parts. Find some negotiating points and tradeoffs to be represented by the common coin. People can more easily swap nickels and days than fortunes and careers; with patience and imagination, the nickels and days that are agreed upon can be pieced together into sizable packages.

5. Bring in facts. They may not be believed at first but persist. Reality can be persuasive; in any event, it eventually has to be faced.

6. Bring in trusted third parties for conciliation, fact-finding, or adjudication. These should be well-known to the bargaining parties, trusted and respected, and they should be skilled and discreet in dealing with sensitive matters. They needn't be superpersons, but they must be known for fairness and talent.

7. Take the easiest problems first. There is a tendency in conflict situations to focus on the major problem first, which is usually touchy for both parties. Start elsewhere; learn to walk before you run. When the parties learn some negotiating skills over the side issues, the bigger problems might be more easily solved.

8. **Keep early discussions informal.** In particular, keep people from digging into firm positions with public statements. Loss of face is involved when people go public; stay discreet.

9. **Emphasize the benefit of shared good feelings.** If you can avoid the appearance of nagging, gently remind all parties of their mutual interest in reaching a sensible resolution. Parties in conflict usually have some shared history worth preserving; help them see that.

10. **Limit each discussion to a few issues.** Don't try to solve the whole problem at one time; that's probably impossible, and it tends to keep tempers high. In particular, emphasize an overall problem-solving approach, rather than thinking in terms of sheer "victory."

11. **Look for, and foster, flexibility.** Continually explore shifts in the way that the parties are thinking about the issues. Don't assume that first positions are fixed. In particular, suggest face-saving ways to be flexible. Sometimes these can be trivial, yet effective; a statement such as "It's Friday afternoon—wouldn't we all feel better getting this point resolved by the weekend?" gives each party a publicly acceptable reason, other

than weakness, for softening its position.

12. **Comment on long-term perspectives.** If and only if it is true, point out to the parties that their long-run survival is not jeopardized by the proposed compromises.

13. **Outline outside constraints.** In some conflicts, if the parties do not agree, an outside force such as a court or an arbitration council will eventually impose a solution on them. If it is possible

and ethically acceptable to do so, have this decision announced in advance. This leads to bargaining on the issues still open and is more productive than proceeding with unspecified threats hanging over people's heads.

14. **Gently personalize the eventual impact of failure.** Again, without nagging, quietly call attention to the consequences of a failure to resolve the conflict. Usually, both parties have something to lose if no solution is found. Make certain, as kindly as you can, that they understand that.

15. **Keep talking.** And then, try again. And then, keep talking.

In every leadership position you may hold now or in the future, something of these Hughes/Williams suggestions can be helpful. They are well worth studying and practicing.

VII

The Frustrations of Leadership

"I have long dreamed of buying an island owned by no nation, and of establishing the World Headquarters of our corporation on the truly neutral ground of such an island, beholden to no nation or society."
Chairman of the Board,
A major U.S. corporation,
at a White House Conference,
1972

"I have so many law suits filed against me that my mother describes me as 'my son, the defendant.'"
Warren Bennis
President,
University of Cincinnati

"I don't rule Russia, 10,000 clerks do."
Nicholas,
the Czar of Russia

Leadership can be frustrating, especially when a leader realizes that there are uncontrollable forces at play. "After all," the leader thinks, "I'm in charge here; I own the football. Why can't I call the plays?" The answer is that a leader never operates in a vacuum; there are always outside influences.

Following is a list of major factors that affect the leader's life; they cannot be ignored but neither can they be controlled. The effective leader realizes that these forces are uncontrollable and, instead of brooding, builds a defensive strategy around each one so that its impact is lessened. Maybe you can't beat them but you might be able to contain them. For the following list, think defensively. (The next chapter—"The Pleasures of Leadership"—will give you a chance to think offensively.)

The History of Your Organization

"Those who cannot remember the past are condemned to repeat it."
George Santayana, Philosopher
Life of Reason

"Those who do remember it will find new ways to screw up."
Charles Wolfe, Economist

Every organization has a history that has an inevitable impact on the choices available to its current leaders, and history cannot be changed. The current impact may show up in only trivial ways: "We have staff meetings on Monday morning because that's when we have always had them." The history may be a substantial control-

ling force: "We use 3 x 5 file cards because that's the size we have been using for the last thirty years; the filing cases take that size, the sorting machines use that size; to change would be unbelievably expensive." The history may have created a culture that is almost impossible to change: "This organization has never had a (black) (white) (male) (female) (Jewish) (Gentile) (old) (young) (non-family member) (Southern) (Yankee) (military) (musical) (bearded) (gay) president and to install one now would be devastating." Or finally, the history may have been literally laid into granite: "The University campus was laid out in horse-and-buggy days; if only they had arranged the Mall differently . . ."

Of course, you can change the course of history in your organization from this point on, but it takes energy and you can only do so many things at once. And while you are fighting one stream of history, battling valiantly against the tide, twenty other historical streams are carrying you on relentlessly.

To counteract the undesirable consequences, you certainly have to understand your organization's history. Your best defensive posture is probably to learn all you can about what has gone before—what has succeeded, what has failed, who wants what changes, where the opposition is. History can defeat you if you don't understand it; it may help you if you're knowledgeable. In any event, it is always there, and may even be the major source of stability in your organization.

The establishment of the world-famous Mayo Clinic in Rochester, Minnesota, by Drs. Will and Charles Mayo makes one of the most dramatic leadership stories in medical science. They had many barriers to overcome, but history was not among them. As their biographer writes,

"Medical biography is full of the frustration and delay suffered by young enthusiasts where the hand of tradition was too heavy and the authority of inflexible seniors too strong. But Dr. Will and Dr. Charlie faced no opposition from an established order. There were no nurses to purse their lips in a prim remark that Dr. Blank had always done it this way, no staff of elders to raise a prohibitory voice against methods in advance of theirs, and no board of well-meaning but ignorant lay trustees to forbid what they did not understand."

Helen Clapesattle,
The Doctors Mayo, p. 298
University of Minnesota
Press, 1941

The Economic Situation

Being in charge is a lot easier in an expanding economy. Anytime you can arrange to be appointed sales manager just before a surge in consumer buying, do it; it will make you look like a born leader. Conversely, if you are superintendent of a school district where voters are blasting your tax rates because of a general disenchantment with the cost of government, no amount of brilliant leadership on your part is going to prevent a feeling of oppression in the air. In such situations, a defensive posture is almost assured, and defensive leaders are hardly ever well-thought of.

How do you build a defensive strategy to protect yourself against uncomfortable changes in the economic situation?

Wise economists have written and spoken eloquently on this subject for years, with the result described in the wry comment, "If all the economists in the world were laid end to end, they wouldn't reach a conclusion." Consequently, I have no economic advice to offer, except to point out that most important decisions are made far in advance of their actual impact. Right now, people somewhere are making decisions that will influence your budget two or three years from now. You had better be well-informed. The best protection against economic change is good data about the future, which means that all leaders, to some extent, must be their own futurists.

Another point closely related to the economic situation is the total amount of financial resources available to you; this is also out of your direct control.

Most leaders inherit a budget from their predecessors. While they can expect some annual increase, it is usually modest—not much more than the rate of inflation—and the typical leader cannot do much about that. With the exception of a sales organization—where an active sales campaign can bring in more dollars—or a fast-growing new technology company with a hot product, or a company with some bonanza such as an oil well, most organizations have stable, predictable budgets that do not change much over time.

If you take over one of these stable budgets, there's not much you can do about the size of it. How you spend it is quite another matter; there you can use some of your creative leadership.

The People to Whom You Are Accountable

A frustration of many leadership positions is that you, as a leader, are never quite certain to whom you are responsible. Normally you might think that you are responsible to your superior— your boss—but this is hardly ever completely true, especially as many leaders do not have bosses.

Here are some examples to demonstrate the complexity of this issue. Each of the following leadership positions has several constituencies and superiors. Consequently, the leader can never be certain to whom he or she is accountable.

1. Captain of a high school varsity athletes club
2. Union steward in a factory department
3. President of a neighborhood association
4. Manager of a retail store
5. Chairperson of a university department
6. Commander of an infantry battalion
7. State senator

8. President of an international professional organization
9. Chief Executive Officer of a multi-national corporation
10. President of the European Economic Community

Let's look at the first example closely to illustrate the point. Say you (or your child, if that's more appropriate) have just been elected president of your school's club for varsity letter winners from all sports. In many high schools, this is a prestigious position, one of the most visible student leadership roles. In this position whom are you leading? Whom are you serving? To whom are you accountable?

1. *The athletes in the club who campaigned and voted for you?* Of course. Without their help, you wouldn't be where you are. Further, they are the people who are going to support you in any actions you may take and back the policies you wish to establish. But you are president of the entire club and you are also leading, and accountable to, those members who campaigned and voted against you.

2. *The non-athletic students?* The student body may be your most important constituency. From them will come the major support for your teams. If you ignore your responsibilities to them, you may have no homecoming rallies, no cheerleaders, no audiences, no school spirit; this can make athletic events dreary.

3. *The school coaches?* Of course. They make important decisions about what happens on the practice and playing fields, so you want to have some influence with them; they had better think well of you. You had better be responsive to them.

4. *The faculty?* Teachers influence who is eligible to play, what time practices are held, who gets special tutoring, and who can leave class early to get the equipment ready. If you want their cooperation, you had better be accountable to them.

5. *The school administration?* The principals and the superintendent control athletic budgets, especially special bonuses like road trips and new uniforms. They also make decisions about issues such as scheduling of games, use of facilities, and the general role of athletics in the school curriculum; obviously you want to represent the athletes well to them.

6. *The school board?* These people are elected by your community to oversee the affairs of the school; everything that goes on in the school is their responsibility. If they don't think well of the athletic programs generally and your club specifically, you've got a problem.

7. *The general community?* The people in the community are your ultimate supporters, both as audiences at athletic events and as taxpayers who finance gymnasiums, playing fields, swimming pools, and the total athletic program. If they do not think well of your club members—the school athletes whom you represent—they are not going to be supportive.

Obviously, many of these constituencies overlap, and you needn't have a separate strategy for each one. If you wish to stay in office and flourish, however, you had best give some thought to how each of them view you.

Eventually you will learn that not only are you accountable to each person in these different constituencies, you are also accountable to their entire social networks: their friends, relatives, children, and spouses. Every administrator knows the value of reacting quickly to requests from within the social network of his or her evaluators. Self-interest is not the only reason for quick response—the normal mechanics of friendship also are at work—but when the superintendent's spouse asks you for an autographed copy of the souvenir program, more than simple friendship is involved.

Your best general strategy is to stay organized, do excellent work, and make certain that this is visible to all of your constituencies.

Cultural Traditions

Leadership never occurs in a vacuum. Around each organization is a culture, a collection of customs, traditions, informal and formal laws. Some cultures are more visible than others and have a more direct impact on organizational structure. The military culture, for example, is highly visible and influential; no military leader can ignore it. Other cultures are more subtle, but their effects may be as great.

Most leaders, in one way or another, have grown up in their own cultures and consequently feel comfortable in them. When this is not true—for example, when an American is put in charge of a large business operation in another country—the results can be stressful. Language, dress, food, working hours, and social practices may all be different from those familiar to the "displaced American." All of the newness must be accommodated at once, and this frequently creates headaches. A capacity to adapt to unfamiliar cultures is essential. Extensive travel can provide invaluable experience for coping with foreign lifestyles.

A specific, uncontrollable cultural force is the rate of technological change, which can create or eliminate entire industries and, of course, their leaders. When pocket calculators came in, slide rules and their manufacturers disappeared. Television wiped out vaudeville, jet airliners eliminated intercontinental rail travel. No matter how good the leaders in these affected industries, social forces helped or hindered them substantially.

What is the proper defensive posture against cultural forces and change? I'm not sure, but I think it involves building a strong, innovative organization with diverse talents. You never know which direction destructive change may come from, so you had better have the widest possible protection. The narrowest, most insular organization is the one most at risk in times of change. Breadth helps.

The General Composition of Your Organization's Membership

"One of the mayor's daily visitors is a city official unique to Chicago city government: the director of patronage. He brings a list of all new city employees for the day.... Nobody goes to work for the city without Daley's knowing about it. He must see every name because the person becomes more than an employee; he joins the Political Machine, part of the army numbering in the thousands who will help win elections. They damn well better, or they won't keep their jobs."

Mike Royko
Boss: Richard
J. Daley of Chicago
E. P. Dutton, 1971

Leaders seldom have much direct control over who is in their group; they usually have to work with the people they are given. Mayor Daley's approach, described above, is not at all typical.

A new corporation president takes over and finds that the work force is already hired, experienced, and settled into place.

A new battalion commander soon realizes that the troops now recruited into the new volunteer army are different from those formerly inducted through the draft, and that a commander has no control over the recruitment process.

A new symphony conductor comes in and finds an orchestra already formed, with

a style of its own, and with contracts that make members difficult to replace.

A new student body president or, indeed, any political leader, soon realizes that the constituency is already defined.

Of course, you choose the group in which you wish to play a leadership role—you don't have to run for office, accept the promotion, or seek the job change—but once that decision is made, you will find that, for the most part, your followers have been selected by factors outside of your control.

Your best defensive strategy here is learning to work with and be comfortable around a wide range of people. Leaders cannot afford to be finicky about the kinds of people they deal with.

The Incompetents in Your Group

One of the most common, recurring frustrations leaders face is incompetent subordinates: "deadwood," "burnouts," "troublemakers," "people who aren't motivated, who are a drag on the rest of us."

Leaders of volunteer organizations say, "The quality of membership is dropping"; "We have a lot of people who are in this for their own ends only", "Do we really have to tolerate this stupidity?"

Frustration usually wells up because, again, the leader slowly realizes that not much can be done. In most organizations, there are too many protections for incompetence: tenure, friendship with the right people, length of loyal service, union regulations, due process proceedings, simple inertia—it is just too hard to change things. Along with this there is the normal reluctance of most people to be nasty to others. No one enjoys upsetting other people's lives, and most managers will go to great lengths to avoid firing anyone. Consequently, in most situations people in charge must learn to live with incompetents.

While a leader usually has some flexibility in job assignment—people can be placed in positions in which they can do the least harm—there is seldom much latitude for outright dismissal. A few organizations don't even have a mechanism for dismissal. I recently worked with a professional organization that had an elaborate procedure for asking a new member to join them in their partnership, but absolutely no way to remove anyone. The president was stumped: "Some of these people came in 30 years ago and haven't had a new idea in the past 29—yet they eat up our resources—what can I do?" Answer: not much, try some developmental seminars and hope for early retirement.

One more point should be made here: you should be slow in labelling people incompetent. Most of us like people who are like ourselves, and the competence/incompetence label sometimes becomes confused with the similarity/dissimilarity label. Your "incompetents" may simply be people with different values, needs, aspirations, skin colors, anatomies, or philosophies from yours. They may not do everything exactly the way you want it done, but perhaps they have talents that you are not aware of, talents that could be useful to the organization if you, the leader, knew how to use them. Most people have at least something to contribute; part of your task is to help them do that. Remember . . . leadership is focusing resources.

This point is crucial in voluntary groups because the worst thing a leader can do is to scare off any members, no matter what their level of competence. You need everybody. In neighborhood associations, school clubs, fraternities, Chambers of Commerce, the League of Women

Voters, volunteer fire departments, and political organizations, maintenance of membership is one of the most important leadership tasks. All members, no matter what their ability levels, need to be encouraged to stay active, even though you may have to suffer through a lot of inane meetings.

"It isn't the incompetents who destroy an organization. The incompetent never gets in a position to destroy it—it is those who have achieved something and want to rest upon their achievements who are forever clogging things up."
Charles Sorenson
My Forty Years with Ford

The Informal Gossip Grapevine

People talk. In an organization, when people are informed about what is happening, why it is happening, and what the likely outcome will be, they talk briefly about it, then go on to other things—their love lives, sports, movies they have seen.

In contrast, if new events are breaking and no one is told why or how they are going to be affected, people speculate. They fret, imagine possible disasters, conjure up the worst. Nothing fuels rumor mills faster than ignorance, and

rumors seldom lead to useful outcomes—sometimes they are disastrous.

In the normal day-to-day life of your organization, people are going to talk behind your back. Even as you are reading this, informal exchanges are going on in your organization. You cannot control them, but one defensive action you can take is to share hard information with your followers—long-range plans, budgets, the results of outside contacts, honest appraisals of your problems—so that they don't have to speculate. The more your followers understand and buy into what you are doing, the more motivated they will probably be to help you move the organization forward, and the less likely they are to sit around dreaming up catastrophes.

The less you tell them, the more they will conjure up on their own, especially if they suspect that you are deliberately keeping them in the dark.

Technical Areas That You Do Not Understand

Up to a certain level in your career, you are not likely to be in charge of technology that you do not understand, but at some point, it will happen. You will find yourself supervising people who are doing things that are unfamiliar to you. They may be running an exotic production process, or flying sophisticated airplanes with automatic navigation equipment, or programming the microprocessors that control your building's heating and cooling systems—the range of widespread technology is great and expanding rapidly.

You will feel particularly vulnerable on this point when one of your subordinates says to you: "We need a new thalomazotic hybrid galitron."

"Why?"

"The old one isn't working very well."

"How much does a new one cost?"

"About half of next year's repair budget, if I can find a rebuilt one."

"And if not?"

"All of next year's budget."

At this point, you will probably arrive intuitively at one of the three defenses available against new technology:

1. *Study it.* Learn what galitrons are, and why they fail. The broader your technical background, the easier this is.

2. *Forget it.* Stay out of the galitron business—leave it to people who understand it. After all, Alexander the Great, Napoleon, and Gloria Steinem never had galitrons and they succeeded—why do you need one?

3. *Trust your subordinates.* If galitrons are essential in your business, and if you do not understand them, you had better find

someone you trust who does understand them, and then defer to that person's judgment.

I saw an example of this process at work recently. I was sitting with a select group being briefed by the top banana, the CEO (Chief Executive Officer). The company deals in exotic technology in which silver plays a major role.

One current problem is that the price of silver is fluctuating so widely on the world market that profit margins are hard to predict and control.

One listener, an eager young MBA, made a sensible suggestion. "Why don't we get into the silver futures market and protect ourselves against these wild fluctuations?"

The CEO hesitated. He was an extraordinarily impressive fellow with an engineering background, and his powerful presence made it clear that he was comfortably in charge of this billion dollar operation. "Well, that's a whole ballgame that we don't understand very well—we're just going to react more quickly so that we can pass the price changes on to our customers."

He was clearly indicating that silver futures was a technical area that he didn't understand, one that he wasn't going to study, and an area of responsibility that he was not going to delegate. As his corporation continues to make money, the decision is right for him and his company at this time.

Elections Conducted by Secret Ballot

This is so obvious that it doesn't require much discussion. If you are in a leadership position where you must be re-elected to stay in power, you are always slightly at risk because you can't directly control the next election—you must campaign continually.

Even the pros lose out; witness this passage from Sir Winston Churchill's memoirs on the eve of his election loss one month after WWII ended:

"I went to bed in the belief that the British people would wish me to continue my work . . . However, just before dawn I woke suddenly with a sharp stab of almost physical pain. A hitherto subconscious conviction that we were beaten broke forth . . . The power to shape the future would be denied me. The knowledge and experience I had gathered, the authority and goodwill I had gained in so many countries, would vanish . . . By noon it was clear that the opposition would have a majority. At luncheon my wife said to me, 'It may well be a blessing in disguise.' I replied, 'At the moment, it seems quite effectively disguised.'"

Winston Churchill
Triumph and Tragedy
Houghton Mifflin Co., 1953

Weather

In the United States, we now live in environments almost totally insulated from the effects of weather: we have air-conditioned homes, cars, and offices, we have domed stadiums, we have enclosed shopping malls, we can take a cab to the airport, alight under a canopy, board an aircraft through an enclosed jetway, fly thousands of miles, and change planes in a variety of airports without ever going outside. We seem to be invulnerable to weather, as if we can ignore nature.

And yet . . . a massive snowstorm hits Chicago, affecting air travel all over the U.S. because planes cannot get into O'Hare airport. An extended heat wave hits a city, requiring extra air-conditioning, overloading electrical circuits. Snowstorms close schools, tornados flatten towns, hail ruins crops, rain cancels county fairs—we are still at the mercy of sudden spells of weather.

We can take defensive steps.

One area in which technical advances have immensely improved the lot of the leader is weather prediction; now, through the satellite camera/TV news show, we have excellent, routine, daily weather predictions, and many organizations take advantage of that information. As forecasts become more accurate, we can plan better (defensively) to prevent the weather from controlling us.

While I was working on this book, I had lunch one day at a seaside resort with a climatologist. I asked him if he worked for the government. "No," he said, "I'm in a private firm; we give individual weather forecasts, along with recommended routes, to ship captains."

"I don't understand," I said.

"Well, for example, say you are captain of a freighter sailing from Baltimore to London. You can choose any one of a number of routes to your destination. For a fee, we will predict the weather over each route during the specific days that you will be sailing, tell you how rough the seas will be, in which direction and how fast the winds will be blowing, and recommend the route which offers the fastest, smoothest passage. Our predictions can save you time and fuel, not to mention seasickness."

"If you don't mind my asking, how much do you charge?"

"Not much really—keep in mind that your ship might be worth $50 million and your cargo another $50 million, and that each day's delay might cost you thousands—our usual fee is about $500."

"That is a bargain," I said, "why don't you charge more?"

He shrugged. "Competition—if we charged more, someone else would get the business—but it is a real bargain." (There's a leader once again subject to the economic situation in which he is embedded.)

In a leadership setting, you can take steps to protect yourself against the impact of weather. As the energy crunch tightens, this point will probably become more important for all leaders.

* * * * *

This chapter has listed ten sources of frustration for many leaders, frustrations created by forces outside the direct control of the leader.

All is not lost. Defensive strategies can be developed to lessen the impact of these uncontrollable forces, and the shrewd leader will find them. But, realistically, what excites most leaders is not the defensive strategies they can build around uncontrollable forces, but the offensive plans they can make for elements they can control. This is the topic of the next chapter.

VIII

The Pleasures
of Leadership

*"I am ending the first week with a fair grasp of my
duties. The job itself is amusing and interesting and
one for which I have four considerable qualifica-
tions—a grasp of the economic situation, considerable ease in written and spoken communication,
some knowledge of politics, and an unquestioned
willingness to instruct other people in their duty."*
John Kenneth Galbraith
U.S. Ambassador to India
Ambassador's Journal
Houghton Mifflin, 1969

Leadership is a heady experience because it
involves power. As Madame Ch'ing said in the
quote that opened this book, it is power that holds
your interest; that's what keeps bringing people
into leadership roles, despite the frustrations listed
in the preceding chapter. Power allows you to
make a difference in life, to have an impact, to leave
something better behind you.

Leaders have control; therefore, they have
choices. The control comes from having influence
over several features of their environment. In contrast to the list of uncontrollable forces in the
preceding chapter, here is a list of ten forces

under the control of virtually every leader from Homeroom President to the Secretary-General of the United Nations.

Control over Your Group's Time Together

Leaders can control the time their groups spend together—in meetings, conventions, seminars, parties, ceremonies, and annual meetings— and this schedule control is an important factor in determining what and how much they accomplish. In some settings, as in a neighborhood bridge club, control over the allotment of time—when and where the sessions are held— is almost the only power. In larger, more formal organizations, control of the agenda usually belongs to the leader, and the adroit selection of topics can set the tone of an entire meeting. In addition, the leader can usually control the meeting time, its location and general structure. Outside influences such as the media, various speakers, splinter groups, or community causes can be either encouraged or suppressed. Colleagues can be publicly praised, dissidents can be visibly shunned, coalitions with other groups can be weakened or strengthened, accomplishments can be emphasized, failures can be ignored, the future can be painted brightly or bleakly, all through control of meetings and their agenda.

A vivid example of this happens every May Day in the Soviet Union. During the annual parade in Red Square, every political observer watches carefully to see which officials are seated on the V.I.P. platform and in what order, for this is taken as an indicator of who is and who is not in favor. The power to arrange the annual seating on May Day can affect what happens the rest of the year in Russian politics.

Even when the leader has virtually no control over the non-collective time of group members, control over their time together is a definite asset. In universities, for example, the president has little to say about how professors spend their days, but the power over the many academic meetings and ceremonies they will attend together can be considerable. Whether anything happens as a result of this power is one measure of the quality of leadership.

Your best offensive strategy here is to learn how to run good meetings and how to most effectively use your group's time. Questions of agenda, meeting time, who presides, who is admitted, and what records are kept are important, and can help you achieve your organizational goals.

Control over the Current Topics on Which Your Group is Focusing

This is an extension of the power over agenda. During the course of a year, most organizations have some version of standing committees, ad hoc task forces, or specially budgeted projects—in general, some special activity that focuses on something current. The person in charge can usually influence these activities, either directly by assigning topics or indirectly through the assignment of committee members. The Personnel Committee can be asked to study the issue of promotion; the Facilities Committee can be asked for a report on audio-visual equipment; the Finances Committee can be asked for a report on travel funds. The nature of the final report may not be under the leader's control, but the choice of the issue under study is usually a leadership decision.

Some organizations have standing committees that control their own agenda, so the leader may have less control over them. Even here, the leader usually has something to say about who is assigned to these committees, so again there is indirect control. One of the frustrations of leadership can be a standing committee that has—by the leader's lights—run amok, digging into areas where they have no business, but this situation is rare, especially as the leader usually has budgetary control over such committees.

Control over topics of current focus also gives the leader considerable power over an organization's future. Future planning is an interesting quandary for leaders, and a politically sensitive issue as well. If future plans involve anything but the status quo, somebody's ox is certain to be gored.

Power over the Budget

Control of the money is a heady, lasting power. What you do with it—for good or for ill—determines much of what can happen in your organization, and the impact may be felt long after you are gone.

In massive organizations such as the Army, the Navy, the Air Force, large corporations, and government agencies, decisions based on budgets overwhelm all other considerations. In cases such as the adoption of pension plans, the selection of a new plant site, or the design of a new building, these decisions, based mainly on dollars, have an impact extending far into the future.

In smaller organizations like county professional societies or sports car clubs, control over the funds available for routine mailings, outside speakers, or annual parties, may be the only real source of control available to anyone in the organization.

I have written in earlier chapters about the desirability of understanding your organization's budget. I'm reemphasizing it here; if you don't understand the cash, you can't control it.

Power over Work Assignments

Leaders usually have considerable power over how a group is organized and who does what. Even in bureaucratic organizations closely bound by traditional work rules, the manager or leader almost always has some control over who is assigned to what task, either at the daily level or over some longer time span. Because the nature of the work itself—running a machine, sorting responses from mail surveys, representing your organization at an international meeting, or working with delinquent children— frequently determines whether or not people enjoy their jobs, a manager also has considerable control over job satisfaction. Some tasks are inevitably more favored than others, so rewards can be distributed in terms of what assignments workers receive.

Power over the Group Image

When you are in charge, like it or not, you represent your organization to the outside world. What you say and do, how you dress, who you spend time with, what letters you write, which activities you participate in, and which speeches you give have an impact on how your organization is viewed by its own members and the outside world. You are its representative. If you are the student body president, you are seen as typical of all students; if you are a neighborhood political leader, people believe that everyone from your neighborhood thinks as you do; if you are a corporation president, your views on labor relations, trade with countries exhibiting dictatorial tendencies, or conservation of clean air will be taken to represent the thinking of the people under you. Because the world's image of a group affects how people react to its individual members, you, by tailoring the group image, can have a substantial influence on how your followers are treated.

Because you are your organization's most important public relations person, you should prepare for this role. What image do you want to convey? How can you do that? Think about it.

Lady Bird Johnson, in her refreshingly candid book on life as the First Lady, emphasized the value of preparation for public appearances:

> "We tuned in on my TV appearance in 'The Week That Was,' which was a catastrophe. It was filmed last week with Nancy Dickerson when I was tired, and it was about as bad as I had thought it was going to be . . . the activities of the week had been good, but in my five minute interview I looked just as old and just as frenetic and just as tired and just as unprepared as I was. If I am not smart enough to get a moral out of this, I am not smart at all. No more unprepared things, no more things when I am not well briefed in what I am going to do."
>
> *Lady Bird Johnson:*
> *A White House Diary*
> Holt, Rinehart and Winston, 1970

Power over Who Joins Your Group

In some situations, this power is obvious and direct: hiring workers into your firm, selecting new pledges for your sorority, establishing criteria for induction of new members of a certified profession. In other organizations—condominium associations open to anyone living in a certain area or industrial trade associations restricted to those working in a specific industry—the person in charge can have some influence on who joins, both by formally setting standards of membership and by informally recruiting new members. This has a greater impact on the nature of the group than any other factor. Over time, you can shape the organization somewhat to your liking through selective recruiting—though you will probably learn eventually that the selection of people "to your liking" is filled with pitfalls. (People seldom behave exactly as you predict.)

Your strategy here is to learn how to select and attract the kind of people who are best for your organization, a truly difficult task for most leaders.

The next chapter talks about the selection of people to work closely around you, your "core group," another pleasant aspect of the leadership role.

Influence over Leadership Succession

Leaders have more to say about who follows them in their leadership positions than anyone else. This control can be direct, as in family businesses where one generation legally hands over the reins to the next, or it may be informal and indirect, as when a selection committee seeking a new leader asks the incumbent for advice about the most important qualities to seek in a successor.

There are exceptions: elected officials who lose an election, corporate executives who are fired, coaches who have had a losing season, TV executives whose programs' ratings have dropped—these people have little to say about who takes over next, and the sense of power loss is acute: "lame duck" is the descriptive term.

Still, because of the way this power is passed on in most organizations, current leaders usually have a say about who comes next. Successful outgoing presidents of any group, from the local American Legion Post to the government of the United States, have direct influence over the selection of their successors, partly because they understand better than anyone else just what forces put them in office, and partially because an outgoing president can lobby both publicly and privately for the new officeholder.

What offensive strategy do you use here? Assuming you think well of your organization, you want the most qualified individual to follow you. And more than that, if you are moving up, your replacement may report to you. Under these circumstances you want someone you can easily work with.

"Theodore Roosevelt, the new President, was [William Howard] Taft's friend and ally. He appointed him Secretary of War and then anointed him as his successor in the White House."
William Manchester
American Caesar
Little, Brown, and Co.,
1978

"American banking leaders were delighted when Paul Volcker was picked [as the Federal Reserve Chairman] by President Carter after he had been enthusiastically recommended by G. William Miller, the Federal Reserve Chief who was leaving to become Secretary of the Treasury."
Time, October 22,1979

Power over Formal Channels of Communication

Leaders of most organizations can influence the information flow in their groups, both internally between divisions and externally to other audiences. Whether you are the captain of the college football team, the executive director of a community development organization, or the manager of a fast-food outlet, you have something to say about who knows what, who says what to whom, and what is written. You can't control the informal network, but you can control the formal channels, all the way from what is posted on the bulletin board to who gives what interview to the newspapers to what items will appear in your annual report. This information flow is powerful because it has so much impact on what decisions are made. Whether budgets are increased, whether new leaders are voted for, whether new resources are secured, whether new products are well-marketed, whether the organization even continues to exist depends to some extent on the information flow and how the leader controls it.

Your best strategy here is learning to communicate well, and then teaching this skill to your subordinates. Good formal communications are a powerful ally.

"Power in the wake of the Depression was waiting to be taken, and Franklin Roosevelt was going to take it, and those in the media were going to be his prime instrument ... God, did he make news! Every day there were two or three stories coming out of the White House. He intended to make the whole federal government his, make it respond to his whim and vision, he did so and in that struggle he became this century's prime manipulator of the new and increasingly powerful media."

David Halberstam
The Powers That Be
Alfred A. Knopf,
1979

The Perks of Power

The trappings of leadership are pleasant, reassuring, and seductive; here are two descriptions separated in space by 12,000 miles and in history by 300 years:

"[The Emperor] lived in the magnificent palaces in Peking, surrounded by high walls and guarded by tens of thousands of troops. Almost every detail of his life emphasized his uniqueness and superiority to lesser mortals: he alone faced south while his ministers faced the north; he alone wrote in red while everyone else wrote in black; the ideographs of his boyhood personal name (Hsiian-yeh) were taboo throughout the empire . . . his robes and hats had designs that no other person might wear; before him all subjects prostrated themselves in the ritual homage of the kowtow; and even the word which he used for "I," CHEN, could be used by no one else."

Jonathan D. Spence
Emperor of China
Vintage Books, 1975
Speaking of K'ang-Hsi
1661- 1772

". . . in Florida, after the election the President-elect [Nixon] asked me to be counsel in the White House for just one year . . . I said yes . . . Then people started making things very comfortable for me. My doors were opened and my shirts were washed . . . some guy from the CIA showed up with reams of secret aerial photographs of China. The Signal Corps offered to install a bunch of color TVs in my house . . . I was involved in picking the President's Cabinet . . . With all those angel wings bearing you up and offering

indisputable proof of your greatness, it's not hard to
believe that you're something special."
John Ehrlichman
in the New York Times

In every leadership position, there are specific, direct, practical advantages of being in charge. At the higher levels, they are flamboyant; presidents, CEOs, general officers, and governors have access to limousines, company jets, executive suites, guaranteed attention from subordinates, introductions to famous people, and invitations to exciting places.

In the middle ranks—division managers, department chairpersons, and mayors—there are large offices, hefty travel and entertainment budgets, preferred parking arrangements, secretarial help, and interesting social invitations.

Even in the youngest, tenderest leadership posts—president of the band, scout troop leader, or intramural team captain—the favors of office exist: freedom to cut class, your own key to the building, or the use of the school van to deliver equipment (and stop for hamburgers and shakes along the way). Shallow and superficial as they may seem, the perks of office can define the difference between a humdrum, workaday world and a comfortable, stimulating environment.

"On the way up to Camp David in the helicopter [for a party weekend] the President turned to me and said, "Do you think you could get used to this kind of life? Pretty hard to take, isn't it?"
Benjamin C. Bradlee
Conversations with Kennedy
W. W. Norton, 1975

The Visibility of the Power Role

Recently I participated in a daylong leadership exercise. It was an artificial scenario, designed to resemble "a day in the life of an industrial manager." There were twenty participants playing parts extending upwards from "plant manager" through "division manager," and "vice-president" to "president." The person assigned to the president's role happened to be older, graying, and distinguished looking; he had a true presidential appearance. I was astonished at how respectful and admiring I felt toward a man who, the night before, had been just another participant like me. Simply labeling someone "PRESIDENT" created a fair amount of respect and admiration. It certainly drew attention; all day long we were aware of who the president was, especially as his speech at the "annual meeting" ended the exercise. In the debriefing day that followed, I still felt curiously respectful toward this stranger who had been my president for a few hours. In the real world, the impact is even greater because the position has some true power; consequently, the force and pleasure of visibility become even stronger.

Group members are always aware of the presence of their leader, and the person in command is usually the first to be pointed out to strangers. A corporation president walking into a far-flung manufacturing operation attracts attention; an admiral appearing at the Officers

Club for Thanksgiving dinner is immediately known and draws a small crowd; the director of the research lab is singled out in the cafeteria for introduction to new staff; the newspaper editor is introduced first to the visiting senator; the captain of the basketball team is interviewed first in the locker room—the world is quite aware of "who's in charge here" and reacts accordingly. People in charge like the attention, or they would never have sought out their positions.

There is no particular strategy necessary here; just enjoy it.

* * * * *

Taken as a group, these ten control levers provide the zing in leaders' worlds. Collectively they provide the power whereby leaders can make things happen. They create the single greatest reward for leadership, the fuel that keeps people going after the needs of fame and fortune have been met, and that is:

relevance.

Leaders are where the action is; what they do matters. Decisions are made, people are brought on board or transferred out, money flows or dries up, programs are started, changed, or dropped, buildings are built, trips are planned, projects are started. This is in delicious contrast to many jobs where the world has a certain, continual grayness every day. Even at its worst, leadership—frequently demanding, chaotic, frustrating, tiring, and unappreciated—is never boring. For most leaders, this escape from boredom is the ultimate fix.

"Management is, in the end, the most creative of all the arts, for its medium is human talent itself."
Robert McNamara
President,
The World Bank

IX
Your Core Group

"There Is no joy except in human relationships."
Antoine de Saint-Exupery
Wind, Sand, and Stars

One of the joys of being in charge arises from the special friendships a leader may develop with close subordinates. Because leadership is inevitably a social activity—with long periods of personal contact, intense interaction, mutual failures and successes—the "people dimension" is a central feature of the leader's life.

The relationships between leaders and those closest to them have all the normal characteristics of friendship plus something additional. Because it is lonely at the top, friendships there are more precious. Leaders like and need them, indeed, sometimes crave them, because conversations with friends may be a major release from the pressure cooker tension of their complex lives. Subordinates value these relationships because of the extra herb, "the essence of power," that spices them.

Members of the group that forms around the leader, particularly visible in examples such as the top administrators appointed by U.S. Presidents—Roosevelt's "kitchen cabinet," Kennedy's "Irish Mafia," Carter's "Magnolia Mafia"—have both more power and more responsibility than do other people who appear to the outsider to hold equally responsible jobs. Others may have the same job titles, be at the same occupational level, or make as much money as this inner circle, but they do not have the special power and responsibility that comes from a close personal friendship with the leader.

Consequently, a typical leader has two types of immediate subordinates:

1) those who are there because of their formal position, and

2) those who are there because of their formal position *and* their PERSONAL RELATION-SHIP with the leader. This latter group is called the leader's "core group."

Their special relationship with the leader defines this group. They may not know each other well, they may spend little time together, they may have no other sense of community apart from their service with the same leader, but over time that too can become a powerful bond.

An example of a "core group" is the inner circle of people that might develop around a factory manager. Suppose he has seven people reporting directly to him—three production supervisors, one engineering supervisor, one data processing supervisor, and a secretary. All of them have formal relationships with the manager and are accountable in the normal sense. But there are always other, informal relationships supplementing the formal ones:

1) One of the production supervisors is a close personal friend of the factory manager; they go out together socially once a month, sometimes with spouses, sometimes alone. In these informal sessions, they talk both business and pleasure.

2) The security guard, who worked under the factory manager years ago when he was still a first-level foreman, is a longtime friend who relays opinions to the manager about how other workers are feeling. They often have coffee together, and once when the factory manager needed a door guard for a large party that his teenage daughter was giving, the security guard came over and helped out. The guard has watched the daughter grow up, feels fatherly pride and protectiveness for her, and continually asks her father, the factory manager, about her. Although their status differs within the social structure of the factory, they like and respect each other.

3) The data processing supervisor is an analytical woman who can always be counted on to look at new situations in a cool, clear manner and to give advice

that is factually based. In addition, she strongly believes in the manager's long-term goals and is one of the few people who will argue determinedly for them, sometimes even with the manager himself. She will not let anything pass that contradicts these goals. The manager knows this, and it allows him to take more and larger risks. He knows that the data processing supervisor will always act as a safety valve, preventing him from going too far. Over the years the factory manager has come to trust her judgment, and checks many decisions, other than computer issues, with her. He has also grown personally fond of her.

4) A young, ambitious junior staff member in the engineering department knows the manager well because they were on a task force last year that required a lot of traveling. Consequently, they had hours of conversation together. They are of opposite sexes and, while nothing untoward happened, they did reach a deep level of intimacy, talking long hours about personal issues. The plant manager, beleaguered by his high-paced life, found these personal conversations therapeutic. The younger staff member had the pleasant experience of suggesting some current organizational changes and seeing them implemented as the result of her discussions with the manager.

5) A former staff member, a close friend now working for a company that supplies raw materials to the factory, is a quick source of information about possible shortages. He doesn't see the manager often, but when they do meet their old rapport returns instantly. They both value the friendship.

6) A former college classmate, another old friend, works for a regulatory agency that monitors the factory's pollution control program. This friend's wife, also an old friend of the plant manager's, works for an executive search firm. She is thoroughly familiar with what kinds of people are

available for hiring, and she understands the problem most managers experience with corporate stress. The plant manager has lunch with her every six months or so, and dinner with both of them occasionally.

7) His office manager has been with him for 15 years, first as secretary, then as administrative assistant, then as a manager in her own right. She is competent, supportive, and a useful buffer from the outside world. She knows everything about the manager's history, including where all the skeletons are buried.

This is a fairly typical core group for a high-level executive. Younger leaders at lower levels also have core groups, though they are usually less developed. Even if you start young, as president of your class, you will almost certainly come to depend on three or four people around you for both practical and emotional support. You will need their help, and you will need them to talk to during difficult times, which is one of the reasons the core group forms.

The Psychological Needs of the Leader

There are three basic reasons why the core group develops; the first is the psychological needs of the leader. A leader's life is chaotic; the pace is fast, the stress can be high, and rewards may seem illusionary. The higher up the ladder, the greater the chaos and the more intense the stress.

In this crucible of frantic uncertainty, the leader needs someone to talk to, some outlet, someone trusted who understands. Leaders are people too, and they need to belong; they especially need to know that others care for them for themselves and not just because they have power. Leaders' jobs require often a business-like stance—they must be relatively skeptical and cautious in most interactions—and they tend to develop personal aloofness, or at least an apparent shallowness. Because they cannot generate much personal warmth in their dealings with most others, they particularly need a small collection of people they can trust, people who will listen to their new ideas. A major reason for the development of the core group is the leader's intense need for friendship and emotional support. Leaders who do not have this support more often suffer from ulcers or other psychosomatic ills.

An Extended Span of Control

The second reason for the formation of a core group is the leader's need for an extended span of control. Anyone in a leadership position is faced with a wide range of decisions, from deciding what time the regular staff meetings should be held and who should attend to allocating funds at various levels ("How much are we going to spend on this year's open house?");

from questions of organizational discipline ("This is the third time he has been late because of drinking—what to do?") to the largest issues of organizational policy ("I'm laying out the plans for next year, I need someone to go around and interview everybody, but it has to be someone that I can trust because whoever does it will consciously or unconsciously impose their bias on the answers that they get").

No one can possibly make all these decisions or take all these actions alone; some jobs must be delegated. Collectively, the quality of decisions made and actions taken will determine whether or not a leader is successful; thus, he or she depends on the core group to take over some of these activities and handle them in a way that will fit into the leader's overall philosophy. The core group's success in doing this will, in large measure, determine the leader's effectiveness.

More Eyes and Ears

A third important contribution of the core group is to extend the eyes and ears—in general, the data-gathering capacity—of the leader. These people alert the leader to developments within the organization that he or she simply doesn't have time to attend to; they sift through the mass of available information and decide what items must be called to the leader's attention.

All core groups perform this sifting function, but their manner of handling it is usually determined by the leader's treatment of the information they bring in. A core group works best when it spreads a broad net and does not distort the gathered information. However, if a leader makes clear over time that he or she does not want certain information, either by never acting on it or by becoming angry when it is presented, the core group will learn to sift these items out. For example, if a leader never wants to know about anyone breaking rules—"I am sick and tired of hearing about students who break the 'no smoking' rule. Can't you quit bothering me about that?"—then the core group will stop informing the leader about that problem. In many cases, nothing will come of these omissions. In others, considerable damage may be done to the organization, and perhaps even to the leader, if there is no early warning system for trouble. Small problems can become big crises when they are ignored.

A second difficulty with this "eyes-and-ears" function can arise if the core group is biased because they are all one sex (or race or age or geographic orientation or major in a university or political philosophy or some similar constriction). Information that is not available to these particular subgroups cannot be passed on to the leader; thus, the information base used for decisions will be incomplete.

There are those who believe that Richard Nixon was so isolated by the nature of his core group

(myopically conservative male Republicans) and his unwillingness to hear distasteful information that he did not understand the scope of the Watergate problem until it was too late; his only option was to resign. Honest appraisals of his situation never got through. He needed a more diverse core group to insist that he deal with unpleasant information.

As Napoleon said, "The people to fear are not those who disagree with you, but those who disagree with you who are too cowardly to let you know."

These are the three main reasons *why* core groups are formed: to give the leader someone to talk to, to expand the leader's span of control, and to serve as extended eyes and ears. Now let's talk about *how* they are formed.

The Formation of Core Groups

Professor George Graen from the University of Cincinnati has spent several years studying the formation of core groups around people in managerial jobs. The following principles came from his research.

When a new leader comes into an assignment not knowing the followers beforehand, as when an executive is transferred into a new district or a military officer is assigned to a new command, core group development goes through three stages:

1) **The initial managing stage.** During this time, the leader instructs and assesses subordinates in the usual way: tasks are assigned and outcomes observed. Over time, the leader notes that some workers perform well, others are undependable. Among those who perform well, some seem to adopt naturally the leader's own approach to problems, that is, they make about the same decisions, take about the

same actions, value the same outcomes, in general, "they think and act like I do."

Consequently, the leader becomes steadily more comfortable delegating responsibility to these people; this means that they move into the core group, especially if they are psychologically compatible with the leader, that is, if friendship comes easily. In this stage the leader usually initiates the interactions.

For most subordinates, a relationship with the superior never advances beyond this stage; interactions are businesslike, dictated by the formal roles each person is assigned. But for those people with whom the leader feels comfortable, who share similar motivations with him, and especially those who have some particular talent or characteristic needed by the leader, the relationship ripens into the second stage.

2) **The mentoring stage.** One easily recognizable feature of this stage is the subordinate's tendency to take more initiative, "to act like a leader," initiating projects, suggesting solutions, taking on responsibility. The follower begins to share in some of the action and excitement of the leadership role, being privy to inside information, exercising more flexibility in work assignments, and feeling the frustrations involved in allocating power and resources. The relationship

between leader and subordinate can now be better understood by considering the leader as a *Mentor* and the follower as *Apprentice Leader*. If the relationship continues to grow and expand, if the Apprentice Leader continues to help the Mentor solve larger and larger problems, if the organizational resources allow it, and if the two people see it as in their best interests, a third stage appears, which is:

3) **The normalization stage.** Here the special relationship becomes normal, and perhaps even formalized in the organization's structure and policy manual. Apprentice Leaders become Special Assistants, or receive some other formal title, recognized as individuals with power in their own right, even as their special relationship with the leader continues. Thus, the secretary becomes an office manager, the bright young analyst heads a new Research Department, the production engineer who can always be counted on to do more is promoted to Production Manager. Their special relationships with the leader become engraved on the organizational scroll. Hopefully, of course, the personal friendships continue to grow and flourish also.

For this progression of stages to occur, several leadership conditions have to be present, according to Professor Graen's research.

1) *The leader has to have some leeway in assigning work.* When subordinates are locked into what they are doing, by restrictions such as tradition, age, tenure, union regulations, or by personal choice, the leader has little flexibility for instruction and assessment.

2) *The leader needs some desirable positional resources* to attract and assign to the follower. These vary widely and include planning power, office and laboratory

space, budget control (especially over salaries and travel funds), access to other parts of the organization, and introduction to interesting opportunities outside the organization. These resources are necessary, in some sense, to "buy" the commitment of a potential core group member. The leader has to have something fairly concrete to offer; personality alone is not sufficient.

3) *The leader must be capable of earning the personal commitment* of the potential core group member; here, personality is important. While the use of positional resources is still crucial, something more is usually involved in earning this commitment. When this "something more" is present, the commitment of the followers is higher than that the positional resources would normally produce; followers become willing, even eager, to buy what the leader is selling.

Regrettably, virtually nothing is known, in a scientific sense, about what constitutes this "something more." Some of it seems to be physical—good-looking, physically robust people have an edge in the "something more" department. Some of it must be sheer competence— we tend to follow, with awe, people who are excellent performers in the tasks that are relevant to us.

It is not just charisma; charisma is not a sufficient "something more." Charisma is most effective when contacts are short, shallow, but intense, which is true in *politics,* especially at election time, *religion,* especially during the annual revival meeting, and *sales,* when the product is an impulse purchase, not a necessity.

Charisma, however, has its limitations, one of which is that it doesn't endure long in day-to-day encounters. Charisma doesn't have much to offer over the breakfast table or in long, demanding committee meetings or late in the evening when everyone is tired, hungry, and sweaty, the coffee shop is closed and the hot water is gone. Over the long haul, when people are working closely together, something more than charisma is necessary.

Usually it is some combination of excellence, forceful self-confidence, and ability to communicate which attracts potential core group members to a leader.

New core groups are most often found in fast-growing, energetic, young enterprises where growth provides "something-more" leaders with flexibility and expanding resources. Core groups are less common in stable, no-growth organizations where a lack of discretionary funds and an absence of new exciting assignments handicaps the leader in attracting competent people seeking broader responsibilities.

On the follower's side, several other conditions must be present:

1) *The follower must have some talent* that is needed by the leader. It may be in a technical field such as marketing or computer operations, in a personal service area such as secretarial work, or in a subsidiary management role which requires the ability to implement the leader's plans.

2) *The follower must be interested* in taking on more responsibility than he or she currently wields, and must have the potential to handle it. People who wish to continue in routine jobs, put in their eight hours, collect their paychecks, and go home are seldom found in active core groups. Ambition, a sense of forward progress, is usually necessary. It is important to note here that people in core groups are not necessarily reaching for the leader's job; they may be preparing for some position that is next in line in their own career progression. A computer expert working under a marketing person may be an apprentice for the next step up the computer management ladder, not the marketing ladder. A secretary working for a scientist might take on greater responsibility, playing an apprentice leader role to the scientist while planning to move up into execu-

tive management in the laboratory, not into a scientific leadership role.

3) *The follower must be committed to the leader,* and show more than the usual enthusiasm for his or her programs. This means putting in extra time, thinking selflessly, arguing for the leader's viewpoint, supporting and expanding the influence of the leader, even at the follower's own expense. Usually these extra efforts will be in the follower's best interests also—anything benefiting the mentor will usually benefit the apprentice—but this will not always be true. Being in the core group requires some sacrifice of self-interest. The leader's program is all-important; if members doubt this, the core group tends to disintegrate.

One of the fascinating threads running through the Watergate case involving former President Nixon and his staff was the erosion of commitment that occurred in the Nixon core group. As the judicial proceedings slowly unwound, staff members slowly realized that their own necks were on the line. They began acting to save themselves in ways that were not necessarily in the best interests of the President. John Dean's book, *Blind Ambition,* is an excellent example of "the autobiography of a core group member." Even the title captures the dynamics at work: commitment, then disenchantment. In the books that the Nixon staff members have written about

Watergate, they save some of their most caustic comments for each other and their leader, especially when the legal pressure changed the informal norm from "we're all in this together; draw the wagons up into a circle" to "it's everyone for themselves; I'm going to get to the Grand Jury first." The breakup of the core group—loss of commitment to the leader—had the powerful dynamics of a multiple divorce.

> 4) *The follower must win the leader's trust.* This is one of the most noteworthy characteristics of the relationships between leaders and their core groups— the feeling of mutual trust. It can be seen in their comfortable working relation ship, usually reflected in easy banter and a minimum of formality, and in the latitude given these favored subordinates in their decision-making. The greater the leader's trust for a subordinate, the greater the unreviewed decision-making power allowed to that individual.

Trust between leaders and subordinates is usually based on some combination of the following:

Similarity. The more similar the backgrounds and personal characteristics of the leader and follower, other things being equal, the greater will be their mutual trust. If they are the same race, have the same educational background,

same religious background, come from the same geographic area, and have the same general socioeconomic roots, they will tend to trust each other more.

A special case occurs when the leader and follower are from the same family. Ignoring those cases where some peculiar dynamic creates familial hostility, trust between family members is high because the similarities are so great. Virtually everything is identical except age, and usually goals are the same, as in family-controlled businesses where everyone profits if the company makes money. Close-knit family groups can create very effective teams because their trust is deep and guaranteed.

Similarity in age produces a different result; instead of similar ages producing the tightest bond, things seem to work best when the leader is older. Few people join or remain long in core groups of people younger than themselves.

Predictability, psychological soundness. In most leader/follower relationships, leaders demand predictability in their subordinates. While that doesn't necessarily argue only for yes-people—some leaders are fresh, lively, and unpredictable themselves, and can tolerate such subordinates—the usual pressure on followers is to conform to a predictable pattern.

One common component of predictability is personal soundness, that is, a healthy, problem-solving outlook on the world, free from personal idiosyncrasies.

This required blend of predictability and personal soundness in trusted subordinates is one reason that dramatically creative people, who are frequently anything but predictable, are seldom found on the leadership ladder. Where creative people are usually found, in universities, research laboratories, and advertising agencies, for example, the people going up the management/leadership ladder are usually among the more subdued. The chairperson of a university department does not take under wing the young, unpredictable crackpot (who, because of creative, unrestrained, wild-eyed thoughts, may accomplish the next true breakthrough) to help make departmental management decisions. A healthy, well-rounded, productive but predictable junior faculty member is much more likely to be the one who slowly acquires the management skill necessary to keep classes meeting, materials ordered, and payrolls met.

Shared History. Some followers sift into a leader's core group because the two individuals have a long shared history. While they may be quite dissimilar—one may be young, the other old, or one black, the other white, or one a conservative Republican, the other a liberal Democrat—they have shared some common history, such as time together in the military, long-term acquaintance through church work, or working side by side in the same organization for many years. In some way, they build up a reservoir of shared experiences which serves, for them, to create the necessary shared commitment and trust.

One implication of all of this is that organizations should give young people early exposure to the leadership process by encouraging their admission into core groups. Schools can put students on policy-making committees, at least as observers; corporations can create "Junior Management Committees" so that young managers can get some flavor of the complexities involved in charting future strategies; families can let children participate early in questions of family investments, job relocations, and general lifestyle. Essentially, these are all apprentice experiences for later core group participation and eventually larger leadership responsibilities.

The core group relationships, and the mentoring role in particular, are usually very pleasant experiences for the leader. In fact, a friendship formed through the core group process can be one of the closest bonds possible. Frequently, both participants thrive on it, enjoy it, treasure it. If you don't have this kind of relationship in your leading activity, you may feel a sense of emptiness. The complexities are to be cherished and encouraged, not feared.

In the long run, deep, durable, satisfying friendships with like-minded people may be the major reward of the leadership role. The importance of this is highlighted in the words of a remarkable man, Berry Gordy, President of Motown Industries; he has built up a highly successful recording company, and has a reputation for encouraging young talent. His comment about friendship makes a suitable epilogue for this book:

> *"One of the most important problems in being an entrepreneur is the problem of happiness after success. Many people might say, 'Hey Baby, give me the success, and I'll worry about the happiness afterwards.' Unfortunately, it doesn't happen that way.*
>
> *"Unless you consider happiness before you consider success, then the manner in which you achieve your success will be something that will destroy you at some later date. Many people, in their rise to success, are so busy running to the top, stepping on their competitors, stepping on their enemies, and saddest of all, stepping on their friends and loved ones, that when they get to the top, they look around and discover that they are extremely lonely and unhappy. They'll ask me, 'Where did I go wrong?' My answer has always been, 'Probably at the beginning.'"*
>
> Berry Gordy
> *The New York Times*
> 14 January 1979